OVERCOMING STRESS

OVERCOMING STRESS

Advice for People Who Give Too Much

Tim Cantopher

WESTMINSTER
JOHN KNOX PRESS
LOUISVILLE · KENTUCKY

Cover design by Lisa Buckley Design
Cover photo ©iStock.com/choness

Library of Congress Cataloging-in-Publication Data
Cantopher, Tim.
[Stress-related illness]
Overcoming stress : advice for people who give too much / Tim Cantopher.
  pages cm
Originally published under title: Stress-related illness : advice for people who give too much.
London : Sheldon Press, 2007.
Includes index.
ISBN 978-0-664-26106-1 (alk. paper)
1. Stress (Psychology)--Popular works. 2. Stress (Psychology)--Health aspects--Popular works. 3. Stress management. 4. Mind and body. I. Title.
BF575.S75C325 2015
616.89--dc23

                                                                    2015002765

Most Westminster John Knox Press books are available at special quantity discounts when purchased in bulk by corporations, organizations, and special-interest groups. For more information, please e-mail SpecialSales@wjkbooks.com.

Contents

To the real Mrs. C.

Acknowledgments

My thanks to Dr. Graham Kidd and Dr. Mike Bristow for their advice and help, and for correcting my misconceptions of their areas of special expertise. Most of all, I thank my patients, who teach me what you can't find in any textbook – knowledge born of experience.

Introduction

'That's it, I definitely won't get there in time for my first patient now. I'm in so much trouble. She was cross with me last time I was 20 minutes late for her appointment. This time she'll be incandescent with rage when I don't turn up for goodness knows how long.' The object of my fear was Ethel, a formidable Surrey housewife who fed on errant workmen and tardy psychiatrists. 'But she'll hang on, just for the hell of it, so I'll never catch up and all the rest of my patients will be kept waiting too, even longer probably while she gives me what for. How could I have been so stupid as to come out without my mobile? I can't even let them know. If I try to get to the payphone the train will leave for sure. I'm such a fool, I knew this would happen. I could kick myself.'

My head sagged, my brow furrowed and my hands fidgeted, mirroring the posture of half of my fellow would-be passengers. The other half sat slumped, looking hopeless, defeated and miserable. I was sitting on the 4:15 at a London terminal, stationary, with no idea if we would move before doomsday, and if not why not. It was ten to five. The one exception in this sorry crew was my friend Steve, a New Yorker who has lived here for a while. He was hopping mad. 'Why don't any of you guys do anything? If this happened at Grand Central there would be a baying mob at the station manager's door threatening to string him up by his balls; that gets them moving. Anyway stuff like this doesn't happen there. People tell you what's going on, 'cuz if they don't, they know they'll get their asses kicked. You guys are so passive.' Then he was off to find the station manager. As he disappeared into the crowd, the train pulled away.

Two stressed nations divided by a common emotion, anger/fear/ recrimination/self-recrimination/stress. Whatever you want to call it. It's all the same thing. It's only how we express it and then what we do with it that's different. Steve and I were both very stressed that day, and we exhibited why stress-related illness is so common in both our cultures. It's a near-inevitable emotion, but many factors influence how we experience it.

Stress is cultural. It isn't what is happening that causes stress. It's what we fear is going to happen in the future. What is most feared varies between cultures, because fear is a conditioned response. That is, we learn what to fear. Most of this learning happens early in our lives, a lot of it at the hands of our parents, though I learned fear from a horrid schoolteacher who thought children should be dealt with like army recruits. Steve, like many New Yorkers, has been taught to fear not being in control. Most of my fellow Englishmen, like me, fear being punished. Our culture favors punishment and many of us spend much of our lives fearing the loss that punishment is. In the past this loss of comfort involved being hit with a stick. Now it is the discomfort of being harangued by Ethel. When my mind is at its most catastrophic, I imagine that, in her rage, she will complain about my sloppy time-keeping to the General Medical Council and I'll lose my license, ending my days in poverty and degradation. This hypothetical future may be extremely unlikely, but if we hear a story just once of someone suffering a fate that has any vague similarity to our situation, we can convince ourselves that it is going to happen to us. Then we spend our whole lives running from this imaginary fear.

When bad things do happen, repeatedly, and we fail to influence the events, the result isn't fear, or stress, it is despair and resignation. That was the response of some of the occupants of my train. They had learned that trains are often late and nobody cares enough to tell you why or how long you may have to wait. It's not fair that these innocent would-be travelers should be the ones blamed by their spouse/children/boss/partner while the train operator worries not a jot, but that's just the way it is, always has been and always will be. I am powerless. The others, like me, predominantly feared being punished. A powerful cocktail for depression and stress. The depressed passengers were trapped in their miserable present, while the stressed ones were being tormented by an unpleasant future created in their own heads and blamed on past unforgivable mistakes. Ironically, it is the latter who end up getting sick with depressive illness, among other ailments, not the ones who look depressed. But more on that later.

The people who taught us to fear, to be stressed, weren't very kind. For their various reasons they taught us that the world is a harsh place and the future is to be treated with trepidation. And we are still believing them. As I berated myself at Waterloo, I was doing the same to myself as the teacher-bully had done to me 40 years before.

Maybe there's another way. Maybe if stress is caused by unkindness and by living in the future, the answers may involve staying in the present and being kinder. To others, but even more, to ourselves.

Much of this book will be familiar to those who have read other books on stress, but there is a thread running through this one that, I hope, will form the main take-away message.

Kindness keeps you well.

Before you read further, though, I should tell you what this book is and isn't. It isn't a comprehensive review of the medical literature on the conditions caused by stress, the psychological theories or treatments in vogue at present or the research on the workings of the brain. Nor is it a cognitive therapy book (one seeking to improve health purely by changing thinking style). There are plenty of excellent books of these kinds available and there's no need for another. It has a bit on some of these things; enough to make sense of our experience of stress and what we need to do to combat it. Mostly, though, it is a distillation of what I have learned from my patients – their experiences, mistakes and accumulated wisdom. I hope it will help you to get better, stay well and get happy.

1
What Is Stress?

Any linguistic pedants among you will be used to tut-tutting when this subject comes up and will no doubt be doing so now. 'He's not talking about stress; it's *strain* that he's describing.' Well, you're sort of right, as the word 'stress' comes from the science of engineering. It refers to a line of force on a structure that is in a different direction or of a different degree from that for which the structure was designed. Strain refers to the response of the structure to that stress. So a bridge is not put under stress by its normal loads, but if heavier traffic than that for which it was designed starts using it, or if heavy winds and tidal waters push it sideways, stressing its weakest joints, it will suffer strain, maybe with disastrous results.

But language is forever shifting and so many people have used the word 'stress' to refer to a reaction to an outside stressor that it has come to have this new meaning. So if this loose use of language makes you stressed, I'm sorry, but that's the way this book is going to be. The stress you may suffer will be caused by my literary laxity conflicting with your love of precision, for which I apologize.

This, then, is how I see it. Stress is experienced when a person is pulled or pushed in a direction that they would not naturally take, or at a pace at which they would not normally proceed, or with an impetus that they would not normally experience. They are enduring a force for which they are not designed.

It isn't just nasty things or excessive demands that can cause stress. Some years ago, when money was worth more than it is now, all the winners of big lottery jackpots over a period of a few years were followed up for a year after their life-changing win. Over 50 percent of them developed a stress-induced illness during the course of that year. How could that be? 'I could cope with a stress like that', I hear you say. I'm sure you could, emotionally, but that doesn't mean that your body, including your nervous system, can.

Types of Stress

Most of us feel stress when confronted with danger, extreme demands or rapid changes. But some people, in contrast, experience stress when their natural inclination to live on the edge is thwarted. So a newly retired soldier would be under stress from being forced into a routine office job and might become ill, having coped with being shot at with aplomb. It's the force stopping you from moving the way you would choose to that creates stress. What we would normally choose varies from person to person, depending on personality, experience and a host of other personal factors. So it isn't just what you face that causes stress, it's also you. Here is a way into the problem then. Whatever ghastliness you face in your life, there is probably something that you can do to suffer less stress, because you can change most things about yourself. Yes, even your personality. I'll show you how to do that later.

Stress isn't always harmful and in any case it's unthinkable that any of us should enjoy a completely stress-free life. I suppose you could be born to wonderful parents, be bright, popular and gorgeous and then be killed suddenly by being hit on the head by an asteroid at the age of 25. My American wife says that in her next life she's going to be born 'cute and dumb', as then everyone loves you and provides for you and you don't see the problems before someone else fixes them. But even then, you'd have to be very stupid indeed not to find something to be stressed about. No, let's be real, we all have stress in our lives. But this doesn't necessarily make us ill. In fact, most of us need a bit of stress to feel really alive and function at our best. It's why people play games. I play golf. It's an infuriating game, it's impossible to master (I've been trying for 35 years and I haven't managed it yet, though I always think I'm close) and it often puts you under stress. I love it. Why? Well, it's partly the context – nobody is going to be harmed if I have a bad round, it's pointless and silly. It's also that there is an end to it. The stress ends on the 18th green and is put into perspective back in the clubhouse.

The Stress That Makes You Ill

One of the most important aspects of what separates harmless stress from the stress that makes you ill is duration. We can cope with a brief period of stress, so long as it isn't too traumatic or overwhelming. The problems arise when we stay stressed for long periods of time, because it's not what we're designed for. We are designed for life on the primordial plane millions of years ago. Natural selection adapted us very well for that environment. Our basic design hasn't moved on a lot since then because few things in our present lives threaten our ability to make it to child-bearing age. In those days life was mostly very dull, interspersed occasionally by short periods of extreme danger or opportunity. If an antelope passes your cave, you've got about 20 seconds to do something about it, or you and your family won't eat for a week. If, on the other hand, you emerge from your cave to be confronted by a sabre-tooth tiger, what you do over the next 20 seconds will determine whether you pass on your genes or not. So we got very good at dealing with short periods of stress. The hormone adrenaline was evolved to cause a range of changes to the body to occur very quickly when the need arises. It does a brilliant job, turning us into finely adapted machines able to fight or to run at the peak of our body's capacity.

Within a few heartbeats, adrenaline, released by the body in response to perceived threat, affects almost every bodily function. The heart beats faster, to pump more blood around the body, we become breathless so as to load up with more oxygen, the blood vessels to the muscles and the skin dilate, to allow greater muscular activity and to lose heat, which we are sure to generate in our flight from the beast that is chasing us and all our nerves become supersensitive as we are going to need all possible acuity in the life or death struggle ahead. In addition, the bowels will tend to open up at both ends, as this can allow a rapid jettisoning of a few pounds of body weight, helpful in running faster and will lay a powerful scent trail. As most of our predators in those days relied heavily on their sense of smell, while we don't, the confusion that this causes gives us a few seconds to find a crevice to crawl into to avoid being eaten.

All highly adaptive if you're being pursued by a sabre-tooth tiger, but little use to you if you're sitting in an office, or a restaurant, or at home.

So adrenaline makes us well-adapted to short-term stresses. The problem is that that isn't the way our modern world is constructed. There are few wild animals threatening to eat us and most short-term threats to life and limb have been eradicated. The threats we face are more subtle, more subjective and much longer lasting. We aren't designed for that. So we suffer the effects of stress, rather than being enhanced by them and the same heightened arousal that protected our ancestors makes us ill. Natural selection doesn't care. Most of the physical effects of chronic stress don't threaten our lives until after the normal reproductive years, and as far as natural selection is concerned we are, by then, disposable.

The Continuum of Arousal

So to avoid the illnesses that stress causes, we have to change our perception. 'I know that it seems that there is a threat out there, but actually there isn't, so no need to fight or flee. Thanks very much, adrenaline, but you're not needed – you can go home now. Don't call us, we'll call you.'

If you don't succeed in bringing down your level of arousal, it will drift upward and that's a problem too. It isn't just how long you are stressed for that matters, but also the degree to which that stress leads you to become over-aroused. By *arousal*, I'm not referring to a state of sexual excitement, though that is undoubtedly arousing, but to *how hot you are running*. You could call this your level of tension, alertness, excitement, enjoyment, exhilaration, fear, panic or whatever. But these words make a judgement about degree and whether the state is nice or nasty. They are all the same thing; if the arousal is nice we may call it enjoyment or excitement, if it is nasty, fear or panic. It's how we experience it that determines the label we give it. But as long-term or excessive over-arousal can cause harm whether it's nice or nasty, that's the term I will use here.

Arousal is a continuum, from zero (unconsciousness or deep sleep) to very high. Figure 1 shows a graph of arousal plotted against performance.

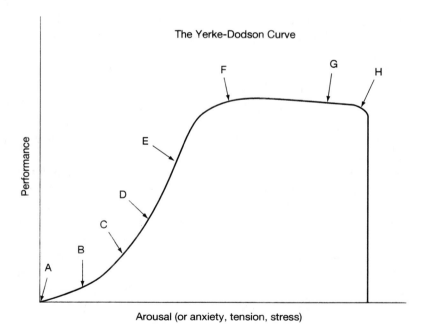

Figure 1 The Yerke-Dodson Curve

This is the Yerke-Dodson curve, named after the two people who first described the relationship between these two variables.

At zero arousal (A) you are asleep, so you can't perform. At very low levels of arousal (B) you can only do very basic things, like making a cup of coffee and some toast. As you get fully awake (C) you can perform basic tasks of daily living but to manage complex procedures you have to be more alert (D), and to work in a demanding and competitive environment you have to be near your peak (E). Then you reach the plateau (F) and you're at your best, really flying, 100 percent. As your arousal level rises further, all seems to be well; nobody would know that there's a problem except you. This is the swan on the water; all serenity above, but paddling like hell underneath. By point G you're in trouble and you'll be feeling as if you're on the edge of a precipice. You are. It doesn't take much more than for you to reach the edge (H) and when the collapse occurs it is rapid. This can take several forms, such as panic attacks, temper loss or just dissembling.

The problem is that it's difficult to keep your arousal level where you want it. You don't often see people at the top of this curve, on the plateau, but you do in top-class sport. The champions don't just have great talent and dedication; they are able to get to the plateau at will. There are no shots or moves that the champion makes that others can't, but he/she is able to make them just when it's needed. If you try to play a tennis match at the top of the curve throughout, you will become exhausted and lose. Most players can have periods of brilliance, but they can't turn it on when it's needed, in the crucial points that decide the match. Anyone who has watched the greats in any sport will know the narrowing of the eyes, the change of posture and the fluidity of movement that comes over them at these times. You know they are going to win and so do they, because they can modulate their arousal level at will.

If you try to stay at the top of the plateau for too long, you will slowly drift up from point F to point G. That's very precarious and whenever anything winds you up, even a bit, you will be unable to function. But many of my patients spend most of their lives at this point on the curve. Eventually they go over the edge once too often and can't get back up again. That is the illness of clinical depression, of which I've written elsewhere and which I'll touch on later in this book.

The key, then, is going to be learning how to run your life from just below the plateau, at between points D and E, popping your arousal level up briefly to point F when you really need to. If you do that it will take a major thermonuclear attack to push you over the edge as you've got so much leeway. That isn't as easy as you would think, as there are a number of factors that are pushing you up the curve and more from your past that got you there in the first place.

I'll turn to these factors now, but before I do, I need to acknowledge the obvious: some people have such terrible and intractable adversity in their lives that there is nothing that I can write that will make things OK. I know that, but I can say this: I see far more people whose stress is at least to some degree chosen, than those for whom there are no answers. It may be worth reading on unless you are absolutely sure that your stress is 100 percent external, that you play no part in it and have no influence at all upon it. And in any case, have you really ever cared enough about yourself to think about running at a pace that you can comfortably and healthily sustain? I doubt it. If you haven't ever given it a thought, because you don't matter as much as others, you need the rest of this book.

2

Present Causes of Stress

Identifying the causes of stress is the tricky bit. There are a lot of causes of stress and types of illness that result from it. But once you have identified which apply to you, you're three-quarters of the way there, because the rest is obvious. Those things you can change need to change. Even those that can't, for example causes of stress from the past, can be addressed, because to get ill, you need to be involved, to be carrying on the damage that others started. So have a look at the causes of stress in Chapters 2 to 4, and see which apply; then you'll find the necessary action that is outlined later in the book follows naturally. The chapters on dealing with stress follow the next three pretty closely. There will be other causes that I haven't included, but the same principle applies – understand the cause and the necessary action becomes clear. You'll find a page reference under the heading of each of the causes of stress that I outline below; this refers you to what you need to do to combat your particular stressors and stay well once you get through your present crisis.

Stress – The Toxic Fruit of Change

(See page 87.)
It has become an article of faith. Change is good and anyone who says otherwise is a reactionary laggard, who needs to be educated or ejected. There are thousands of books on subjects such as 'building a successful organization by facilitating change'. I think this is one of those peculiarities of history, like the belief that the earth was flat or that crops failed because of the malevolence of witches. We now know that those beliefs, held as truth by most of the population at the time, were a load of old tosh. In the future, our reverence of change will, in my view, be seen the same way.

Change is sometimes necessary – indeed, progress wouldn't happen without it – but it also causes harm. Like surgery to correct a bodily disorder, change is an injury, that should only be inflicted when there is no other way of getting the job done. And you had better be sure that making major changes in an organization is necessary, because they will cause stress; and stress demotivates and crushes creativity. It would be one thing if changes in organizations only happened slowly, by considered osmosis, but in our society they tend to happen repeatedly, by ill-considered revolution. So teachers aren't allowed to get on and teach, but must absorb one bureaucratic fad after another, each new structure being tossed aside after a few years for a new flavor of the month. Those who want to teach, rather than to be bureaucrats, feel stressed, with all the consequences that I will outline later. Even more important for our children is that each change reduces the teachers' ability to teach. The same is true, sadly, for most organizations in our modern world. If last year's strategy isn't working to accomplish whatever we wanted it to accomplish, let's try something else this year! Progress! Hurrah! Let's ignore the fact that the stress caused by applying these changes inhibit our chances of success, and probably did last year as well, which is why last year's strategy didn't succeed!

But the truth is that this isn't a new phenomenon. It has always been so, because it is part of human nature. To illustrate: 'I have come to realize that repeated change produces a wonderful illusion of progress, while all it actually achieves is widespread demoralization and demotivation.' This was written by Caius Petronius, commander of a Roman legion, in AD 33.

Most leaders feel the need to change things, in order to make the organization their own. It's like a new homeowner wanting to redecorate their house, or an animal marking out its territory with urine. It says, 'This is mine'. People want a purpose, to feel that they make a difference. Those in positions of power feel this more than most, and are able to put their wishes into practice. The trouble is that the difference they make is usually for the worse. It's like a process of natural selection, with most changes not working and dying out, but once in a very long while, one change makes a real improvement and stands the test of time. So society moves forward, but at a terrible cost to those of its citizens who care enough, try hard enough and are sensitive enough to try to make every change work.

Bad Things Are Not Allowed

(See page 88.)

The second phenomenon that leads to escalating stress in our modern society is the belief, encouraged by our politicians, that nothing should ever go wrong. Every time something really bad happens, the search is on for a scapegoat. Once some unfortunate soul is sacrificed in the name of 'accountability' we all feel better. Then a quango is set up to make 'reforms'. More change, more forms to fill in, more stress, less achieved. Again, I can't see this changing in the near future, because the promise of preventing bad things from happening keeps politicians feeling important. It also keeps good people feeling afraid. 'I won't shape up, I'll be found out, I'll miss something important and be out of a job.' People thinking this way don't perform well and they get ill a lot.

Getting More for Less

(See page 89.)

This is something that almost every employed person has experienced over recent years. Each round of redundancies is accompanied by increased targets for those who remain. Everyone is pushed to their limit and then a bit more. In some industries this would seem to be inevitable, as there is apparently no other way to compete with the developing world, where salaries are so much lower.

The trouble is that pushing people beyond their limit is only a short-term solution. In the longer term, it leads to a demoralized and therefore inefficient workforce. My prediction, for what it's worth, is that industries that compete in a market where skills are not required will cease to exist in this country before long, as you can't compete with companies paying ten rupees an hour, however hard you push your workers.

However, I'm noticing an opposite trend in some forward-looking companies. I do a bit of work for some of the American multinationals. They used to be the worst at flogging their workers to an early grave, but not any more. In the past they ran toxic practices like '360-degree appraisal', in which each year you are assessed by your boss, your peers and those reporting to you. In my early days in psychiatry I treated scores of casualties of this system. How can you make the difficult decisions and say the difficult things a manager sometimes has to, knowing that your livelihood may depend on keeping everyone sweet? Rhetorical question; you can't. So they dropped the system (true to form, a U.K. agency is now considering introducing it, but that's another story). Go round the offices nowadays of one of these companies at around 6:30 p.m. and you'll find managers sending people home. They realize that their best employees will do whatever is asked of them and more, but at the cost of escalating stress that, in the end, will lead to illness. This doesn't make good financial sense, so limits are imposed on how hard people should work. This is by no means universal yet, but I think I see a trend.

It isn't just how much you are expected to achieve that determines whether or not you will get ill. It's also how empowered you are to achieve it. While we all would love to have power without responsibility, more often we are faced with the opposite. If you increase the demands you put on a person without giving them the means to achieve them, you will make them ill. Conversely, if you empower someone, through increasing their authority, resources or feeling of effectiveness (self-esteem) they will be able to achieve sometimes amazing results. Again, some companies are realizing this.

In any case, you can only do what you can do. If you try to do the impossible for long enough, you'll get ill. So a woman with a young family and a demanding job tries to be the best mother, employee, wife, daughter and friend that has ever been and becomes ill. A doctor or a teacher tries to carry through all the latest bureaucratic fads demanded by our misguided politicians and to be a really good doctor to her patients/teacher to her pupils. Impossible. She becomes ill. I've treated and retired so many of our best public servants who've been burnt out in this way, it's depressing. But as I will explain in Chapter 7, it's avoidable.

I've had to realize this myself. In my own way, through magazine and newspaper articles, interviews, lectures and responses to government consultation documents, I have tried to limit the harm that I can see being done to our public services by excessive bureaucracy and change. But I have come to realize that I will fail, because I exist at the wrong time in history, when the press, who set the public agenda, isn't yet interested in calls for the damage to stop. So I'm giving up the fight, satisfied that I've done what I can, ready to get involved if an opportunity arises to make a difference, but for now directing my creative energies elsewhere.

Stress Is an Illusion

(See page 91.)

So our environment is becoming ever more stressful and it looks like we're stuck with it. We're all going to experience the effects of stress, then? Well no, not necessarily, because while these external factors are outside our control for now, it needs more than these for stress to harm us. More important even than all the unpleasantness that life can throw at us are internal factors. That is, the way we think, feel and behave in response to these circumstances. We can do something about those. The internal factors with which we hurt ourselves tend to mirror the external ones that the world throws at us, as I will make clear. Maybe that isn't so surprising, as we're all products of our culture.

In one way, stress is an illusion, created by our minds to fit in with the way we view the world. How often does the catastrophe we fear actually occur? Most of us carry a degree of fear most days of our lives, lest this or that misfortune may occur. If even a small proportion of these calamities actually came to pass, we would be candidates for 'the unluckiest person in the world' and be in the newspapers. Bad things do happen to us from time to time, together with a sprinkling of good things, but both tend to fall out of a clear blue sky and not be what we fearfully predicted. In any case, in my experience, and I've seen a number of victims of misfortune, it isn't the thing we most fear that determines whether or not we achieve happiness in our lives. I've met people who have lost their job, marriage, house, sight, limb or anything else you can think of achieve a contentment that most of us can only dream of. In contrast, many of my most anxious and unhappy patients have never suffered any major misfortune or loss.

The illusion of stress is fed by our attempts to predict our future. We feel the need to nail down the future, to keep it where we can see it. Sometimes we try to barter with it. 'I can accept that I may not get the promotion I'm hoping for and which I've worked my fingers to the bone for, just so long as my family remain healthy and my daughter gets into college.' Unfortunately, life has no interest in your bargaining and will do exactly what it chooses, regardless.

It is this need to be in control, particularly of the uncontrollable, that seems to fuel stress and the illness it causes in those affected by this affliction. It's as if life were a bus tour. This person can't just sit back and enjoy the ride. Instead he has to leap up, push aside the driver, and

take over the controls. Sadly, if you do this, you won't experience any of the interesting scenery, because you're so busy steering the bus. Life is a lot less interesting if you're trying to control it all the time.

Indeed, the author of the best-selling book on human behavior *Games People Play*, Eric Berne (I recommend that you read it if you haven't already), says that you aren't truly alive if you spend your mental time in the past or the future. He gives another automotive example, of a man driving a car and arriving at a jam. He curses himself for taking this route and worries about the consequences of his delay (like me at the station). Neither of these scenarios – his culpability in arriving in his current predicament or his imagined future – are real or alive, says Berne, because they are selectively edited and he can't do anything about them. Essentially he is dead. What distinguishes the animate from the inanimate is the capacity for action. Much better to stay in the present and devote all of your attention to navigating a route as well as you can. Then when you reach your destination, you can deal with whatever you find, not having wasted your energy along the way on what you can't influence.

Many others warn against straying too far from the present. Eckhart Tolle, the author of *The Power of Now* (also recommended), reckons it is the cause of most modern ills. Alcoholics Anonymous call it 'projection' and warn that failing to 'keep it in the day' causes unnecessary stress, leading alcoholics to risk relapse. This doesn't mean that you shouldn't engage in reasonable planning, just that you shouldn't waste your time and energy in a hypothetical future. I'll come back to this later, as my task in this chapter is to outline some of the present causes of stress, not to give the remedies, which come later. For now it's enough to establish that spending too much time in the future or the past makes you ill. Worry won't work.

Nothing Must Ever Change

(See page 91.)

While we are pulled this way and that by the changes our leaders foist upon us, many people have a powerful intolerance of change in themselves or their lives. You never allow yourself to change your mind as a result of experience. That would be 'making a U-turn', so derided by politicians. How often do you hear one person in a dinner party argument say, 'Yes, on consideration, I'm persuaded by your argument. You've helped me to see things differently. Thank you for helping me to become wiser.' No, what you witness is two combatants beating each other over the head with predetermined opinions that have as little chance of shifting as those of the Reverend Ian Paisley. It's a pity, as the fear of being shown to be wrong, or to shift one's opinion, does a lot of harm, causes us a lot of unnecessary stress and keeps us as ignorant as a politician.

Equally, many people spend a lot of time fearing that the good things in their lives will be lost. This can, in some of my more anxious patients, fill their every waking minute with dread. Well yes, in the end you are going to lose everything, even your life. Along the way, though, good things will happen, as well as bad. Life is full of entrances and exits. It never stops. Finding a way of accepting the changes that life delivers is a very large part of combating stress.

Conflicting Needs

(See page 92.)
One stress does not usually make a person ill. Most people are pretty resilient and can shoulder a heavy burden. It is when two mutually incompatible needs collide that the trouble happens.

- I need more rest, but I need more money.
- I need some time for myself, but my children need to see more of me.
- I ought to spend more time with my parents, but they put demands on me. They don't realize how much I have on my plate.

There are a hundred and one of these and they all produce the worst type of stress. It's not just the irreconcilable nature of the needs either, it's also the context.

I have little time or energy left after I've finished my day's work, so I thought it would be a good idea to go away with my wife to a sunny resort to write the bulk of this book in a calm, peaceful atmosphere, away from the day-to-day stresses of my job and home. It didn't work. On the third day of writing I felt very peculiar. Being in the business, I quickly realized that I was having the symptoms of a panic attack. Fortunately, I've learned techniques that allow me to deal with such symptoms quite rapidly, but this event surprised and shocked me. I love writing and I loved the place at which we were staying. What was the problem?

It was this: the process of writing requires quite a high level of arousal – at least it does for me. The other purpose of the trip was to rest, recuperate and slow down after a challenging few months. These two needs were incompatible. My body warned me of this. I took note. Most of this book was written in rainy old England.

Taking Responsibility for the Happiness of Others

(See page 92.)
It's not just the workings of society, the past and the future that we can't control. It's an irony that many of my patients spend most of their lives focusing on what they can't control, while ignoring the things they can. They feel that they have responsibility for every-thing and everyone. 'Something must be done! This is something, so I must do it', is their refrain. This comes into the most stark focus in their relationships with friends and family.

It's one of the better aspects of human nature that we like to make people happy and to make things right. That is, most of us do. The truth is that most people are quite nice, most of the time. Most of us have our off days when we're grumpy and our selfish side, which comes out occasionally when our particular needs are threatened, takes center stage, but most of the time we recognize that the needs of others matter as much as our own. I think that about 90 percent of the population is like this. The other 10 per-cent, though, is split into two groups: those who give all the time and those who exclusively take. The takers acquire, over time, a collection of selfless individuals upon whom they feed, making increasing demands upon them.

If you are someone who can't bear anyone being unhappy with you, you will, over time, be surrounded by these parasitic types, who I will describe in more detail later. Before you know it you'll be organizing, doing work for, ferrying around, visiting, lending to, bailing out and apologizing for more people than you can shake a stick at. It's a matter of time before your rising arousal level leads to illness.

I'm sorry to have to tell you this, but you will never achieve what you crave, that is, the love and respect of those whose demands you service so faithfully, because they aren't able to give these things. They don't know how to. They can only take. The answer, hopefully, is obvious, but I'll come to it later. Chapter 4 deals with some of the people who harm you.

Communication Problems

(See page 93.)
This subject deserves a separate book. I may get around to it some day. Communication problems between good people certainly cause more stress and unhappiness than external problems do. And they are avoidable. I will only touch on these issues here, but the book *Games People Play* by Eric Berne that I mentioned earlier tells you a lot more, as do John Gray's *Men Are from Mars and Women Are from Venus* and the follow-up *Why Men Don't Listen and Women Can't Read Maps* by Allan and Barbara Pease.

Not all relationships need to be or should be intimate. By *intimate* I mean saying what you really mean, sharing your real thoughts and feelings. With your partner this may lead to physical intimacy too, but I'm talking about intimacy of communication. Most relationships need a bit more distance than this for the sake of kindness and safety. The unkindest and most stressful people are those who are inappropriately honest. They excuse hurtful barbs such as, 'Are you sure that top is wise for someone of your age?' or the like, by calling them 'helpful feedback', or declaring, 'I'm just straight talking; I call it as I see it.' I'll talk more about such people later, but the point here is that honesty, or intimacy, is only appropriate in certain situations.

In a really close relationship, such as a marriage, though, intimacy of communication is crucial. You need to say what you mean and what your needs and wants are. You need to recognize that your partner (if he/she is) is of the opposite sex and that men and women think differently. If a wife expects her husband to be intuitive and predict her needs without having them spoken, she will usually be repeatedly disappointed, because however civilized he is, he's a man. If a husband expects his wife to consider emotive issues dispassionately, with a coldly linear logic, he's probably in for a rough time.

So the best close relationships are intimate, and they are also *spontaneous*, meaning that you say what you mean *at the time that you mean it.*

If honest, spontaneous and intimate sharing of feelings and needs fails, bad things happen and stress ensues. A relationship may become distant, dominated by formality and ritual, or at its worst, deteriorate into 'game playing'. That is, a set of covert manoeuvres designed to force your partner into a position he or she wouldn't otherwise accept.

'What do you want to do for your birthday, darling?'

'Oh, I don't mind, whatever you like.'

So she sets up a low-key dinner for the two of you, at which you are grumpy.

'What's the matter?' she asks, to which you reply: 'Well, it is my 40th. I might have hoped for something a bit special, like a party or something.'

An argument ensues, during which you have an opportunity to offload all the resentments you have built up over months, through not telling her what your needs and wants are. She would never have agreed to an argument if you had asked her for one, but you've neatly foisted one upon her. The pay-off for you is that you temporarily feel better. When you've made up you will probably even justify what happened as 'clearing the air'. But you're not, you're poisoning it. Before long she'll start doing the same to you, or she'll retreat into her shell and any intimacy will be gone. It's a horribly stressful way of leading your life.

A bit of game-playing happens in most close relationships, but if yours is based mostly on this type of communication, you're in trouble. You, your partner, or both, will probably be experiencing one or more of the effects of stress. This type of system is horribly stable and can last a lifetime, so unless you do something about it, it isn't going to change in a hurry.

I Must Never Fail, and Other Thinking Errors

(See pages 88 and 100.)

People run too hot because of the way they think. Cognitive therapists spend their time finding the negative thoughts that lead people to run too hot, then looking for the deeply held underlying assumptions that lead to these harmful thinking patterns.

A typical negative thought leading to stress would be: 'I'm going to fail at my job.' The underlying assumption might be: 'I have to do more than others to be OK', or 'I'm no good', or 'I'll be found out/wanting' or any variation on any of these. A nice example of such thinking is the ditty:

> Out of the gloom a voice said unto me:
> 'Smile and be happy, things could be worse'.
> So I smiled and was happy and behold
> Things did get worse.

That makes me titter. Unfortunately, some of my patients believe it. You should never be too happy, as life will play a trick on you and bring you crashing down. Better be secure in your pessimism, then you'll never be disappointed. True, but you'll never be happy either and your disappointment-free life will be a waste of time.

This is about the way you think. Those who see the world, themselves and the future in a negative light suffer a lot from stress. Let me give an example.

Upcoming layoffs are rumored in a company. John has a positive view of himself. He feels that it's a privilege to know him and he sees the world as a good place in which, even when bad things happen, things turn out for the best in the end. He doesn't fear redundancy as he expects to get another job quickly should it happen. As a result of lack of fear, he is able to keep working creatively.

Paul, in contrast, thinks catastrophically. At the first whisper of redundancy he expects he will be the first out. He doesn't think he will get another job as he doesn't think he is up to much. His mind races forward and he sees himself and his family starving in abject poverty. He is paralyzed by fear, is unable to concentrate on his work, falls behind on targets and, as a result, his fears are realized. It didn't need to be so.

There are several other types of negative thinking problems that lead to stress. These include *overgeneralization* (one thing went wrong, so everything will always go wrong); *selective abstraction* (the ten good things said about you this week count for nothing; only the one passing criticism you received matters); and *black and white thinking* (unless I'm always perfect, I'm useless).

Some therapists see the emotion of shame as being the driving force behind these thinking patterns. Shame certainly does seem to have a very destructive influence on many of my patients, leading them to ignore their needs in favor of a headlong pursuit of blamelessness. A desire for perfection can be rooted in deep shame. Whether or not you ever see a therapist, it's worth stopping to think what you are like. Maybe ask a good friend. You may be viewing yourself very differently from how others do.

I see this slightly differently. What I notice above all in my patients is a particularly vicious form of self-criticism. Like a bully, they lie in wait for any mistake they might make, then when it happens, they attack themselves with relish. They would never do this to anyone else; they aren't bullies. They reserve this mental beating for themselves. As a result, when any challenge or decision arises, they are paralyzed by fear. They know that if they get it wrong, they will punish themselves horribly. This is ironic; while we have decided that punishing children too harshly is not a good idea, since they don't learn this way, we are tending to punish ourselves more. It's as if you were standing over yourself with a stick, looking threatening and saying, 'You'd better get it right, because if you make a mistake I'm going to beat the living daylights out of you.' We don't do that to kids any more, having learned from the mistakes of the generation of teachers that taught me, but we have no compunction to doing it to ourselves.

I first noticed how disabling this is at one of my favorite places: the cricket pitch. I won't name the focus of my learning, as that wouldn't be fair. Suffice it to say that, even if you are a follower of cricket, you won't remember him, because he didn't make it at the top level. This batsman was top of the county batting averages. He

was in a class of his own. But when I saw him walk out for his first scrimmage innings, I knew he wouldn't succeed on the big stage because of his demeanor. You could see before a ball was bowled that he cared too much, that he was too afraid of failing. So of course, he did. Repeatedly.

This problem is often misunderstood. American sports commentators in particular tend to talk of the competitor who just falls short being 'afraid to win'. No, he isn't. He's scared stiff of losing, because he has just realized that he might win and that victory might change his life. The thought of failure terrifies him, because he's already assumed the benefits of victory and now fears losing them.

Fear of failure leads to stress and therefore to failure.

Value Judgements

(See page 96.)
Value judgements are statements including words such as good, bad, should, shouldn't, magnificent, pathetic, brave, feeble and

the thousands of others that declare our evaluation of a person, their actions or attributes. In my view a value judgement tells you nothing other than what are the values of the person making the judgement. They are useless, but they are also worse than that. They squash creativity and create stress, particularly when we make them about ourselves.

'I'm so pathetic. I'm not even able to cope with bringing up my family. I should be grateful. I've got a good husband, wonderful children, a better house than I deserve and no real stresses. Lots of my friends cope with much more, do more than I do at home, hold down jobs and look better than me, without ever complaining and they never get ill. I'm so weak.'

If I've heard this lament once, laced as it is with unflattering value judgements, I've heard it a thousand times. It causes my already-sick patient to get even iller because of the guilt and hopelessness it engenders. And it's so unfair, because it's selective. You've selected, as the group to which to compare yourself, the most energetic, highest achieving and prettiest people you know. And they haven't told you that they have someone to clean their house, leave their spouse to deal with the kids after 7 p.m., take a nap every afternoon, and only work 12 hours a week. You're competing with a myth and punishing yourself for losing.

We get accustomed to using these judgements about ourselves, especially if our parents used them a lot. It's very difficult to stop it. At least it is until we start treating ourselves with the respect we accord to others. More of that later.

Alcohol and Other Drugs

(See page 96.)
The mind-altering substances that we use to try to feel better are both a cause and a result of stress. They are also major factors in turning stress into illness.

The problem with drugs, or at least the addictive ones (this includes alcohol and tobacco), is that they reverse their own effects in the long term. You can predict the long-term effect of addictive drugs by looking at what they do in the short term. The long-term effect will be the opposite of the short-term one. Then when you try to stop taking the drug you suffer an even greater opposite effect. This is a withdrawal syndrome.

Take alcohol, for example. You are feeling stressed, anxious, low in mood, lacking in confidence, are sleeping poorly and have a lot of aches and pains. You have a couple of drinks and hey presto! These symptoms all disappear. What a wonderful drug. Except that the effect is short-lived and you don't realize, because the effect is so small, that your symptoms are just a little worse each time the booze leaves your system. Thus a slow drift occurs in the opposite direction to the effect that alcohol has each time you take it.

Look at the graph in Figure 2, which is of just one such symptom, anxiety. Imagine you start drinking regularly to combat your anxiety at point A, because you are more anxious than average. The slow drift upward occurs gradually and by the time you arrive at point B you are in real trouble. If you carry on drinking, there is no limit to how high your anxiety level can rise. It will happen slowly at first, but more rapidly as your consumption increases, which it inevitably will, since it will take more and more drinks over time to control your anxiety the way a couple did at the beginning. If you stop drinking, your anxiety level will rise very rapidly, though only

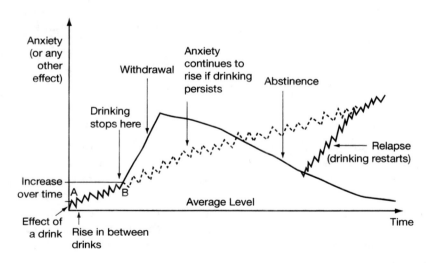

Figure 2 The Opponent Process

temporarily. Either way, you're in for a bad time; you are trapped. This is addiction.

The same will happen with any drug that works immediately to reduce the effects of stress. It won't happen with antidepressants because they take weeks to work and are not addictive (more on this later). It happens pretty rapidly with cigarettes, which have the added complication of stimulating production of the body's stress hormones and causing a number of other changes to the body which increase the harmful effects of stress. Don't believe anyone who tells you that cannabis is harmless and non-addictive; it isn't either of these. Apart from its other harmful properties, it has the same effect of slowly ratcheting up anxiety and other stress symptoms as does any other rapidly acting tranquillizer. Any benzo-diazepine (the Valium group of drugs) and related sleeping tablets are just as bad. While many people think that sleeping tablets are less addictive than tranquillizers, in fact the opposite is true, as a sleeping tablet is really just a tranquillizer in higher dosage. If you take a little of such a drug, it will make you calmer to begin with but slowly more anxious. Take a higher dose regularly and you will sleep at first, but experience more rapid increase in anxiety as well as insomnia over time.

Any other illicit or recreational drug will have an even worse effect. Beware anything that carries the promise of a short-term fix to anxiety and other stress symptoms.

Lack of Balance

(See page 98.)
This sounds like a cliché. Your life needs to be in balance. It's remarkable, though, how many of my patients have lives that are lacking any balance at all. You can be the brightest and most determined person in the world, but if you don't get any exercise, your career success is going to be brief. Exercise is a powerful stress-reliever. Without it you won't be able to handle the stresses you face for many years. So while taking the time to go for a run or a walk may feel like time and money wasted, it will help you to achieve more in the long term. If you are already ill, however, for example with clinical depression, don't force yourself to do

anything vigorous just yet; in severe depression pushing yourself in this way can make you worse. Wait until you're better first.

The same is true for every other aspect of life as for the balance between work, rest and exercise. For example, if you give everything of yourself to your kids, parents or friends and take nothing for yourself, if you spend every available minute improving your mind, or going out, or crafting or trainspotting, you'll be at risk of getting ill from the effects of stress.

I started this chapter looking at some of the ways our culture makes us stressed and ill. It won't have escaped your notice, though, that each of these external threats to our well-being is mirrored by a similar assault that we launch on ourselves. We can't easily change our culture – not alone and overnight, anyway. But we can treat ourselves more thoughtfully, as valuable commodities to be protected, at the very least.

I will come back to each of these points later, when I look at how to deal with stress. For now, it's enough to say this: STOP BULLYING YOURSELF.

3
Past Causes of Stress

Genes

Some of my patients fear almost everything. In particular, they fear that a disaster will occur which will be their fault. Even when they have no influence on a situation, they will still blame themselves when it goes wrong.

A good example of this is genetics. The woman in a state of stress-induced anxiety or diagnosed with depressive illness fears less for her own future than that of her children. She assumes that her genes, lurking in her children, are a curse that has already condemned them to be affected in the future, as she has. It will be her fault when they do and she is already punishing herself in this certainty.

OK, putting aside the unfairness of blaming yourself for genes that you didn't choose, let's get this into perspective. Your children's genes are less important than their experiences through childhood. You can do something about the latter, but not the former. The psychologist H. J. Eysenck said in the 1950s that, in psychological development, environment is twice as important as genetics. I think that's about right. Some conditions have a stronger genetic component, but those caused by stress seem to be caused more by poor experiences and faulty learning than by genes.

It is quite difficult to separate out what is caused by genetics and what by childhood experience, because a child bearing his parents' genes is also usually brought up by them. But it isn't impossible. Studies of identical twins, particularly reared separately, have allowed these relative influences to be teased apart.

The bottom line is this: A child born to parents who have experienced stress-related illness is more likely to develop such an illness than are the general population. But a child who witnesses a parent briefly become ill with such a condition, then get well and stay well, is not enormously more at risk than is anyone else. Indeed, they may benefit from seeing the parent change his thinking and actions so as to become more healthy and happy.

Concentrate on getting well and learning how to stay well. Children only need to be loved, approved of and taught consistently and kindly, which I'll come on to shortly. You'll be able to achieve this if you are well and happy. So stop worrying about your genes.

Personality

(See page 98.)
There has been a lot of research on the relationship between personality and stress-related illness. It has been shown that those people who run most hot, that is at the highest level of arousal (stress, tension, excitement – it's all the same thing) have the highest incidence of developing stress-related illnesses. This isn't really very surprising, when you think about it. The term 'type A personality' has been coined to refer to these competitive, driving types who demand a lot of themselves.

I think the more interesting questions are: What is personality? Can it be changed? What choices can someone with this personality type make to avoid getting ill or getting ill again?

Given the caveat that I made in Chapter 1 about people in terrible situations, I can say this: *stress doesn't make you ill – you do.* Give a stressful situation to someone who is weak, cynical, lazy or manipulative and he will immediately give up, or get someone else to do it, or won't care, or will moan and groan so much you do it yourself. In any case, he will never get stressed enough to get ill. The 'type A' person, on the contrary, will tackle the situation head-on and will demand that he successfully overcomes it, without help. But what if the situation is un-overcome-able? He'll just keep going until illness stops him, which eventually it will.

About 35 years ago I researched various psychological measuring devices as part of a project. One of the tests purported to measure persistence. It involved me cutting a piece of blank paper into randomly shaped pieces, mixing them up and then asking subjects to arrange them back into a rectangle. However, unknown to the subjects, I removed one of the bits of paper prior to giving the rest to them, so the task was impossible. The measurement to represent 'persistence' was how long the subject continued to try to solve the puzzle before giving up.

Two of the subjects stick in my memory: my aunt and my mother, who I had co-opted as guinea pigs. My aunt, a formidable lady who had no time for anything or anyone who didn't amuse her, gave up after 17 seconds. In contrast, I had to stop the test when my mother, in tears of frustration, sweating and puce of complexion, was still at it three hours later.

Some things can't be fixed. If you try to fix them, you'll get stressed, then you'll get ill.

Back to the questions I asked above. I see personality as nothing more than a product of your behaviors. If you say someone has an 'outgoing personality' you mean she goes out a lot. If she's an 'introvert', given the choice, she stays in. We often make the mistake of assuming that these behaviors are an entity in themselves, explaining everything. Some years ago a particularly clear-thinking judge criticized psychiatrists (quite rightly in my view) for our circular thinking. 'When asked why the criminal employed the criminal behavior they reply "because he is a psychopath". Then when asked what is a psychopath, they reply, "someone who behaves in a criminal fashion". That's of no use to me.' I agree.

Personality is merely a description of behaviors and can change at any time. Sure enough, people behave the way they do for a reason, but that doesn't mean that they can't change the behaviors should they choose to. If they do so for long enough, they will also change the way they feel and think. For example, if an introvert wants to become more extroverted, he can if he acts in an extroverted way for long enough. He'll need some help as he won't know how to do it at first, and he'll be acting, but that won't matter in the end because of the basic psychological principle that *you become the way that you act*. I'll come back to this later. The same is true for 'type A' people. They can change by making different choices and behaving differently; tricky at first, but easier as time goes on.

Parents and Other Problems

(See pages 100, 105 and 107.)

Those of you who have read my book *Overcoming Depression: The Curse of the Strong* may remember Jane. She is the apparently privileged child whose parents, being industrious, provide everything for her. Except for praise, which is a shame. Children don't need much to grow up happy and healthy, but they do need this: to know that they are loved, needed and worthwhile. Her parents have everything organized and so Jane's five-year-old efforts to please them with gifts of her artwork are not welcome.

'Yes, very nice dear, now clear it away, and come and have your supper.'

'But I made it for you, Mummy,' she complains.

'That's enough, do as you're told and stop making a mess. Your father will be home soon; he'll be tired and we don't want to upset him by spilling glitter on the carpet, do we?'

So Jane diverts her attention elsewhere. There's not much attention to be had at home, so she puts hers into schoolwork. As a result, she comes top of her class in her first exams. At the end of term she comes home clutching her report card, expecting the usual dismissal from her parents. But she doesn't get it, because her success reflects on them; she's a chip off the old block, her success being the result of having such brilliant parents.

'Oh, my goodness! You came first! You're brilliant! We must phone Nan, Aunty Norah and all our friends to tell them. We'll be one up on the Joneses across the street, always on about their precious son and his scholarship. You'll beat that, just you see, you'll graduate from Cambridge and have a brilliant career. Oh, how wonderful!'

From this moment Jane is hooked. She has to have more of this lovely praise. It becomes the way she defines herself and the way others define her: the clever one. But what if she isn't really super-intelligent, but just averagely bright, succeeding mainly by pure effort? The answer is that she will succeed, because you can achieve a lot through effort. For a while. She'll take the SATs, struggle through AP classes, though suffering some symptoms (which her parents will ignore), and get into college, though not, to her parents' dismay, Oxford or Cambridge. She struggles, but eventually graduates, without honors. Her parents are disappointed, which is a crushing blow to her. She vows never to let them down again.

She joins a company and rises fast, by doing everything that is asked of her and more. But eventually she rises to a level where her peers are much more gifted than she is. They can achieve more than her with half the effort. She's there until the early evening, but still struggling to reach her targets. She gets her first poor appraisal and is told that she'll have to do better or consider whether this is the right job for her. By this point she's also married and has a two-year-old daughter. She feels guilty that she leaves the child so much with a nanny. Her husband is dissatisfied that she's home so late, is tired all the time and isn't interested in sex any more. She is neither the perfect wife, mother or employee.

Jane is trapped in a hell-hole. She wants, no, *needs* success. It's who she is. And she needs approval. That has always been the only way her self-esteem is maintained. But that's exactly what she can't have.

What can she do? Well, what she's always done. She's overcome every obstacle up to now by pure effort. So she tries the same again. She works even harder and later, making it up to her daughter by playing with her more at the weekend. She does all the chores at home to placate her husband, also doing her best when she can stay awake to be a sex goddess.

This isn't possible and it isn't sustainable. But she does it anyway, because it's all she knows how to do. She can't bear the alternatives of failure and disapproval.

So she gets ill, with one stress-induced illness or another; it's inevitable. Blessed relief! She takes sick leave. But she uses the time to do more at home, so she doesn't really get well. She returns to work not much better and so doesn't perform. The whole ghastly cycle starts all over again. The end points are several, but none of them are good. Divorce, dismissal, problems with her child, misery, illness; often several of these in any order, and perhaps even death.

And all because her parents were too busy being important to understand that a child doesn't need much, but she does need attention, unequivocal love and approval.

Incidentally, I've given an example using the pursuit of academic excellence here, but it could just as well be achievement in sports, being thin and pretty, being the best housewife or whatever. What matters is that parental expectations are met; the form this takes depends on their values.

I see this background history several times a week. But I see another, arguably even worse, pattern even more often. That is of parents who are so self-obsessed that they don't give their child anything emotionally at all, however well she does. But they make enormous demands on her. In truth, she takes more of a parental role than do her putative parents. She looks after her younger siblings while her parents are at the bar, she does many of the chores, isn't supported much in her homework, and is used as a confidante by her mother when her parents fall out, which they do often.

It's one of life's saddest ironies that lousy parents gain the undying and devoted attention of their offspring throughout their lives, while really good, loving and attentive parents are lucky if they see their adult sons and daughters two or three times a year once they have left home. The reason is obvious. Good parents bring up children who are confident and outward-looking. Once they are grown up and have left home they are far too busy interacting with the world to have much time for boring old parents. In contrast, if you neglect your kids and only focus on your own needs, your offspring will lack a sense of self-worth and so will be constantly craving your approval. As adults, these unfortunates will still be doting on their parents, ignoring their own needs and limits. The tragedy is that they will never get the love and approval they so assiduously seek, because their parents wouldn't know how to give it even if they were so inclined. They have always focused exclusively on themselves and now this pattern is deeply ingrained. They are, in a way, emotionally disabled. But their son or daughter doesn't acknowledge this, feeling that to think of their parents this way is disloyal. So on they go with their hopeless and thankless mission, getting more and more stressed as time goes on. Then when one or other parent dies, there's only their offspring for the other one to turn to...

It isn't just parents who can oppress you, though they are best placed to do so. Some people develop stress-related illness even though they have had wonderful childhoods and great parents. Others, seeing everything negatively, either as cause or effect of their depression, selectively remember only the worst aspects of their childhood. So as a parent of a stress-sufferer, don't assume it's your fault. In any case, there are many other people and circumstances who can have a lifelong effect on children.

Teachers, for instance. It is one of the main areas in which our society has improved that teachers no longer hit children; in fact many of them actually use encouragement rather than threat to get their pupils to learn. In my day it was a bit different. While some teachers were lovely, one or two were a threatening presence, standing over us with a stick, ready to beat the living daylights out of us if we made a mistake. One, a horrid old bully, insisted that if anyone made a mistake in the multiplication tables, he must declare his 'carelessness' in class and then present himself for a beating at its conclusion. The temptation was to keep quiet. But this teacher would walk around the class and audit the self-marking of a random selection of pupils. If you had hidden your error, you would be in for a much more terrible thrashing. To declare, or not to declare, that is the question. Shall I, shan't I? Do I dare?

Perfectly designed to produce a class of high-achieving nervous wrecks, which, I believe, many of my peers are. But if this type of sadistic bullying messes up kids, so it does to adults. Sadly the victim of such childhood adversity tends to punish himself mercilessly when, as an adult, he makes a mistake.

Life can do it to you anyway. Adversity through parental illness, misfortune or death can do a child much more harm, through persuading him that the future is to be feared, than it does to an adult who has hitherto had few really bad experiences.

Learned Helplessness, Learned Helping and Other Mis-learning

(See page 105.)
When I was at medical school there was much less concern for animal welfare than there is now. We were set to perform various experiments on laboratory rats that seem terribly cruel by today's

standards. One of these involved a rat in a cage containing a bar at one end and an electrified grid for a floor. The grid gives the poor animal a shock every 10 seconds, but if the rat presses the bar it will switch off the current for the same period, thus avoiding one shock. The rat, not being a very bright creature, takes a while to figure this out, but eventually does so by chance and learning the consequences of his actions. Eventually he learns to press the bar once every 10 seconds. By increasing the frequency of the shocks and reducing correspondingly the time the bar press switches off the current, you can get the rat working really hard.

Then you change the rules. Now the bar is uncoupled from the electricity supply so that the rat can't stop the shocks, however furiously he presses the bar. For some time he increases his efforts, but eventually he gives up, lies on the floor of the cage and lets himself be shocked.

Now you open the door of the cage, take the rat out and put it on the floor. Then you let in a hungry cat.

Under normal circumstances, the rat would be out of there in the blink of an eye, but this time he doesn't move. He lies on the floor of the laboratory and waits to be eaten. This apparently inexplicable behavior occurs because the animal has learned to be helpless. It doesn't matter what I do, I'm powerless to influence my environment. The normal rules mean nothing, so I have to accept whatever is going to happen.

This can happen to humans too. The earlier you do it, the more profound the effect, but the principle is the same. Persuade a person that he has no influence on his environment and what happens to him, and he will become helpless. Torturers in military dictatorships understand this and use this knowledge to gain power over their victims, through making reward or punishment independent of their prisoner's actions. Inadvertently (I hope), successive governments are doing this to public employees through repeated 'reforms'. But it's much easier to do it to a child; all you have to do is be inconsistent, failing reliably to reward desired behaviors or avoid rewarding bad ones. So a child treated irritably by her tired dad one day, having behaved well, and then rewarded the next by her guilty dad, having behaved badly, will become a person who feels powerless in the face of a chaotic and frightening world.

A child needs to be certain of being loved, whatever he does. If the love he receives is contingent on him being useful to his parents and others, he will learn that his only value is as someone who helps. As I have outlined, that will make him very vulnerable in the future to those who would take advantage of his good nature. Of course, there is a balance to be struck here. Nobody wants to bring up selfish children who have no sense of duty or community. Life is full of balances to be struck and this is one of them. Lack of balance in this regard, one way or the other, leads to illness in the individual or those around him.

OKness and Cognitive Dissonance

(See page 100.)
We learn most things when we are young. To me a child is a blank computer disk. Childhood is about loading the operating system and the primary programs. By the time you are 18 or so, the programs are more or less in place. You can alter them later, but it takes quite a bit to do so. A child absorbs things naturally. I think there are three main programs that every child needs. They are: 'Education', 'I'm OK' and 'The world is OK'. Education is obvious; you need to learn some stuff to get by in the world. But even more important, you need to learn that whatever happens, whatever you do or don't achieve, whatever anybody says about you, you are OK, *because you are you*. Whatever happens, good or bad, it'll be OK in the end, because the world is an OK place. If you learn these lessons, you have a happy life, unless you are really unlucky and suffer wave after wave of misfortune later in life. You absorb most reverses with phlegmatic acceptance, because of your happy and realistic underlying assumptions. But if you don't, you tend to run your life as a set of threats to guard against, hostile circumstances to overcome and people to please.

It's a matter of time before you overload. Life is OK when everything runs well, but you will be very vulnerable to adversity. You will look like a strong person and indeed in many ways you are. You never give up and you achieve and overcome everything. Until the smelly stuff hits the fan; then you demand too much of yourself, overload the fuse and eventually cause it to blow.

Cognitive dissonance

Cognitive dissonance refers to the distance between your real self and your ideal self. The little chap in the cartoon is lifting weights. He imagines that this way, one day, he will become the hunk that appears in his thought bubble. No, you won't! Look, mate, you're a scrawny little weed and you won't look like that if you pump iron from now until doomsday. But you're a great guy: kind, charming, amusing, loved by friends and family and admired at work. Give it up, concentrate on your strengths and avoid pulling a muscle, as you surely will if you carry on.

The smaller the distance between your ideal self and your real self, the healthier and happier you will be. This is a simple but crucial principle and a central part of many therapies.

Childhood Adaptation

(See pages 72, 91 and 106.)
Kids will cope with anything. They are ultimately adaptable. Give a child a situation that is unbearable and she will find a way of tolerating it, sometimes in ways that an adult who didn't face childhood adversity would be unable to manage. For example, an abused child may create an imaginary situation in her mind, in which she is safe

and loved and all adults are kind. This imaginary world gives her comfort and allows her to tolerate the intolerable. She may create imaginary friends to help her. She may imagine that she is in a different place, or not in her body, or not prone to pain or other feelings. She may even, in extreme cases, create other personalities within herself who are able to cope with each situation she faces. Such a child will be noted to act out of character at times, to be detached, in a dream or 'not herself'.

In a horrible situation, this child is using her young and unformed mind's ability to adapt to good purpose. It allows her to survive.

But what if bad things keep happening over a long period? These adaptive mechanisms will become ingrained. Once adult, a person loses the flexibility to change her ingrained adaptive strategies, because they become unconscious and automatic. So she finds that whenever she is under stress or perceives any threat, she flips into the same state as when she was suffering as a child. The trouble is that now it doesn't work. Whether she just becomes blank and passive or develops a more extreme reaction (such as in what Americans call 'multiple personality disorder' and British psychiatrists call a 'dissociative state', or dissociative identity disorder, in which apparently different personalities may emerge in response to trigger situations), she won't react to her situation in any effective way. As she withdraws into her internal world her problems grow through lack of action, leading to more stress, more withdrawal and so on.

Most people who experience these automatic reactions to stress feel very ashamed of them and so don't talk about it, fearing that they will be called crazy. It's a shame; they are not crazy and the problem can be resolved through psychotherapy, of which we'll discuss more later.

Some people repress their feelings on purpose, believing that difficult emotions and situations are better off not discussed. While this may not have quite the same immediately damaging effect on your life and relationships as the types of complete emotional withdrawal I've just described, bottling up your emotions will harm you in the end. You repress your feelings at your peril, because they don't disappear, they just turn inward and build up, temporarily hidden, but lurking, ready to be released in an uncontrolled and sometimes damaging way when life turns hostile. Your mind is a pressure cooker. If feelings aren't dealt with on the surface, the pressure builds up, until something breaks. In any case, your feelings mean something. They need attending to and their implications need to be worked out. The alternative is illness.

Trauma and Loss

(See page 106.)

There's a lot of research showing that trauma and loss lead to stress-related illness and that early events of this kind are even more harmful than later events. For example, a girl who loses her father before the age of 14 is at much higher risk of stress-related depression when faced with adversity later in life, such as being let go from work, than one whose parents survive her childhood. The idea that adversity breeds strength is false; early adversity makes you more vulnerable.

Why should this be? Surely losing your job can't be equated with the death of a parent? But actually it can. Both involve a loss of security, comfort, certainty, role and value; the world is no longer a place that can be depended on, where good things happen. The young girl copes, in the way, as I have explained, that all children do, but she internalizes a bleak view of the world. This lies dormant while life proceeds OK, but when she gets her pink slip, she gets a double dose of loss, past and present, and is now at risk of being overwhelmed. In the future, moreover, she is going to be constantly on the lookout for situations that may bring more loss. If grief or depression is our reaction to actual loss, anxiety or stress is fear of loss in the future.

Learning to Fear

(See pages 100 and 105.)

Like all animals, we learn from our experiences. We develop schemas about the world based on events in our lives: models that allow us to explain what has happened and predict what will happen in the future. We also learn a lot vicariously from our parents. If they are fearful and overprotective, and overreact to things, so will we tend to act similarly when we grow up, passing on those same traits to our children. Then if we have an adverse experience, we can easily become paralyzed by fear by avoiding the object of the experience. If you are bitten by a dog, all you have to do to become phobic of dogs is to avoid them for long enough.

So learning to fear is about the way we think and view the world, but also about how we act. Confront the object of our fear and the fear lessens. Identify and confront our negative learned patterns of thinking and it lessens even more. This is the basis of most therapies for stress-related illnesses, of which we'll discuss more later.

4
Toxic People and Places

(See page 107.)
People are the worst stressors of all. While it is undoubtedly true that the best experiences in life come from our relationships with others, so do the worst ones. Though you can change a hateful job, though time heals losses and traumas, pernicious people are always there, digging away at you, pushing until you go under. Many of my patients with stress-related illness have one or more illness-inducing people in their lives; often several. My patients are mostly the good, diligent givers of the world. Most people are quite nice most of the time anyway, but a small minority aren't. They are on the lookout for people like you, those they can take advantage of. They've got sharp antennae, and if you don't actively keep them away, they'll find you. Before you know it you'll be surrounded by these takers and would be excused for thinking that most people are selfish, critical and undermining. They aren't; it's just that these ones are, and you're letting them use you.

Here are some of the types of people who make you ill. I alternate the sexes in my descriptions, but of course these people can be male or female and come in all shapes and sizes. These are typical examples, but give me a bit of dramatic license. The person who is making you ill may have characteristics of a number of these personality types, but not conform exactly to any one of them.

Boundary Invaders

This is someone who pushes and challenges any limits put in his path. Your generosity will be taken as a right and the start of negotiations. At first this can be engaging and amusing. He will breeze into situations which ordinary people find intimidating and take charge. He says outrageous things and gets away with it. He gets discounts in shops when there is no sale on.

But slowly this person will extract more and more from you, subtly shifting the boundary forward every time you give ground. Before you know it you will be giving him more than you can afford, and be exhausted from chasing around for and after him. When you try to impose a limit, to say no, or to excuse yourself, he will be offended and harrumph off in high dudgeon. If you tell a little lie to pretend you aren't available for whatever task he has set you next, he will move heaven and earth to find you out and will confront you publicly with your perfidy. You soon learn that it is easier to do as he asks to keep the peace. But where does it end? In illness, when you succumb to the effects of the stress he has caused. Then he'll blame you for not being there for him and will imply that your illness is 'all in your mind'.

If this person is your parent, he will remind you frequently of the debt you owe him for bringing you up, and indeed for life itself, conveniently forgetting that he didn't do much other than criticize and intimidate when you were little. But if you please him enough, even now, maybe, just maybe, he will one day express his love and appreciation...

Dream on.

Chaos-Producers

These chaotic people career through life like an out-of-control juggernaut, leaving a trail of distress and destruction in their wake. This person will arrive in your life like an explosion, grabbing your attention with her immediacy and vitality. She grabs your affection with an intensity that takes your breath away.

The trouble is, this doesn't last; and when she stops telling you that you are the most wonderful person in the world, she will attack you with a ferocity that is scary. If you cross her, she will hurt you in whatever way she can. If she can't hurt you any other way, she will hurt herself, for example by taking an overdose of medication, leaving a note explaining that it is all your fault. The act will usually be timed so that she is discovered in time, or she may phone you to tell you what you made her do. Occasionally this goes horribly wrong: if you come home later than expected, or she has taken tablets (such as acetaminophen) that she wrongly assumes won't kill her.

Life with this person is a continuous cycle of drama and crisis. Exciting at first, eventually scary and very, very stressful.

Users, Abusers, Loafers and Energy Vampires

The user is your opposite and you attract him. He fits snugly into the space that your generous, trusting and giving nature provides. He takes whatever is on offer, without feeling any obligation to give back. His sense of entitlement is limitless. If you let him, and you usually do, he will take everything you have. This individual is usually also abusive. Not necessarily physically abusive, though he may do that too, but always abusive emotionally. By this I mean that he treats your feelings and welfare with contempt. If he is feeling like it, he may be charming; but if he is irritable or upset, he will have no compunction at all in taking it out on you. Indeed, whatever he feels or wants, he will do to you or get from you.

This includes sexual abuse. While only a minority of users and abusers are sexually abusive, there is a lot more of it going on than you would think. People who sexually abuse their or other people's children are at the extreme end of this category, with the most pronounced personality traits. This isn't surprising, as sexual abuse of children is a big boundary to cross. For a person to persuade himself that he should act in this way, he has to employ some fairly powerful psychological strategies. Prime among these are denial, rationalization and blaming. 'I didn't really do it; it was just a misunderstanding; my innocent affection was misinterpreted,' or 'It was just a brief aberration caused by stress; I wasn't thinking straight,' or 'The kid seduced me, egged me on; I was a victim of her wiles.' All these are typical statements of the sexual abuser. Instead of taking responsibility for his actions, he will justify them or try to lie his way out of trouble. He deliberately ignores the truth that children aren't responsible; responsibility comes with adulthood. He will use all his manipulative skills and experience to intimidate and force compliance from his child victim, persuading her that if she blows the whistle, she will be blamed.

Many forms of abuse are more subtle than this and can be perpetrated on people of any age. But what all abusers have in common is the wish to have their way and have you bend to their will.

The 'loafer' is also abusive, but in a passive way. He is a user who relies on your conscience, standards and perfectionism to get out of having to do anything. He will often use humor to excuse or hide his sloth and you will find yourself the object of his barbs. He assumes that you are there to carry out his wishes and uses your tendency to put yourself last to get what he can and to avoid putting anything in. He really is a waste of space, but somehow he gives the impression that you are lucky to have the privilege of serving him. Because he isn't actively nasty, he tends to slip under the radar. Other people like him and will take his side against you, because he is charming and persuasive. It may take you a long time to realize how much harm he is doing you, but don't be fooled; he will harm you. In due course he will use you up and as likely as not, once he no longer finds you have much to give him, he will cast you aside without so much as a thank you. It's all about him.

The 'energy vampire' is a kind of loafer. He finds you because you are caring and give of yourself. He will give you a tale of woe that goes on and on. When you suggest a solution to any of his problems he says: 'Yes, but I can't do that because...' This is also a type of game (see below). Its purpose is to hold your attention and to get you to hold the feelings that the vampire doesn't want to deal with. But he tells you that you are special, the only person who really understands him. You start by feeling angry with the people who have let him down and caused his problems. This makes him feel better, as someone is feeling angry for him. But then, slowly, you realize that he is blaming one person after another for his problems and doing nothing to solve them himself. You begin to feel frustrated with him yourself, but that only increases his neediness and the emotional demands he puts on you. He will be on your phone or doorstep all the time, his tearful distress more dramatic by the day. He won't stop until he sucks you dry.

Manipulators and Gameplayers

I mentioned gameplaying in Chapter 2, but it deserves another mention here, as some of the most toxic people use games as their weapons of choice.

We all play games from time to time. It's a normal part of human nature. By a game I don't mean fun and frolics. The games I'm talking about are no fun. A game in this sense is a covert set of interactions designed to put you in a position that you would not voluntarily have occupied. I described a game in Chapter 2 under 'Communication Problems'. This one had a husband putting his wife in a position where she would let him down, allowing him to take his anger out on her in order to feel better. There are an unlimited number of games and they all cause stress to the person on whom they are played. In the best relationships they happen hardly at all; in the worst, they are the daily fare of life.

All of us have occasionally played a game of this type. Most of the time, though, we are transparent and reasonable. The gameplayer, on the other hand, spends her life playing games, in order to bend people to her will. She will have become expert in getting her way by covert means. She is exhausting to be around for long, but very difficult to escape from, as she will be adept at making you feel guilty. If you find yourself feeling guilty a lot, but can't quite work out what you've done wrong, you may have one or more gameplayers in your life.

Guilt is also the weapon of the manipulator, who is a subtype of gameplayer. She uses the application of guilt exclusively to get what she wants. 'I've been feeling very poorly for weeks now and you haven't visited me once. I can't get down to the shops, I'm so weak. I can't believe my own daughter won't even take the time to help her sick mother. I'll probably starve, then you'll be sorry.' So off you go to the other end of the country again, to do her bidding one more time, even though you've developed stress-related illness yourself and are, in truth, far iller than she is. She has made you ill and always will, but you daren't tell her as you don't want to upset her. After all, she's old and frail. What if she were to die after you fell out with her? You'd never forgive yourself.

She's got you.

Aggressors and Sadists

There's really nothing you can do with aggressive people. As it says in the poem 'Desiderata': 'Avoid aggressive persons; they are vexatious to the spirit.' That's about the size of it. You can't argue, rationalize or negotiate with an aggressor, because he isn't motivated by sense, fairness or even gain. It's no use appealing to his better nature because he hasn't got one. What he wants is to dominate you, to bend you to his will, and he won't take no for an answer. If you try to disagree with him, to resist his demands, to question or challenge him, he will get increasingly angry and aggressive, until you give way or retract. He always gets his way, or there's hell to pay. Sometimes he may be violent. If he is and you threaten to leave him as a result he may, for a while, become apologetic and promise you that he will change. It won't last, though, because his frustration and need to subjugate will eventually become overwhelming. Aggression is who he is.

Sadists are a particularly scary subtype of aggressor. The sadist is mainly motivated by the need to hurt and humiliate. He gets off on your pain and distress. He relishes hurting you in any way that he can, whenever the opportunity arises. While some sadists are criminal, as in the sexual sadists that populate many crime novels, most are much more subtle than that. He may have fantasies of sadistic sexual practices, but he won't act them out as he wouldn't like the consequences of getting caught. Instead he uses everyday situations – words, humor, judgements and positions of power – to cause you the pain and humiliation that he so loves to witness. He is often charming and persuasive. He gets your trust and often gives you a lot, at first, apparently out of pure goodwill. But beware; once you have accepted his beneficence, he has a weapon with which both to enslave you and to hurt you. Maybe he has bought you expensive meals and jewelry, apparently asking nothing in return. Then he starts criticizing you in public, making you the butt of his jokes and pointing out all your shortcomings. If you have ever confided in him any secrets about which you are ashamed or embarrassed, he will store these up and throw them back at you when you are at your most vulnerable. He can be terribly hard to get away from, as he's very clever at binding you to him. He knows how to make your life hell and he will stop at nothing to do so if you cross him. When you do leave him, be he a friend, lover, business partner or acquaintance, he will go to extraordinary lengths to try to reel you back in. Don't be deceived; if he has taken pleasure in hurting you once, he will do so again, if he can get you back in range, because that's what turns him on.

Addicts

The addict, whatever her drug or behavior of addiction, doesn't care about you. All she cares about is how to get her next hit. It makes no difference if she is an alcoholic, a drug addict, or is addicted to gambling, food, dieting, exercise or sex. She may have been the most wonderful and caring friend before her addiction took hold, but once it has, her addiction is everything to her and you don't even come a poor second. If you threaten her addiction, she will attack you ferociously, or drop you with a callousness that takes your breath away. She may profess love, respect or affection, especially when intoxicated, but in truth she is unable to love. Love is about selfless giving; she can only take.

If you spend a lot of time with her, you will be changed. Without realizing it, you will start facilitating her addiction and losing sight of your needs, rights and wishes. Living with an addict is an awfully long life, so bleak, so dull, so unrewarding and sometimes so dangerous. She will use you up, then, when she has got what she wants from you, she will spit you out.

I won't go into addiction in detail here as it is the subject of many other books (including one of mine). In any case, there is a free resource available to you at the end of the phone, in the form of Al-Anon, the sister organization to AA, for the partners and families of alcoholics. Every addiction has its equivalent to AA and to Al-Anon. They will give you all the advice you need. I will only add this. Addicts who are in recovery can become wonderful people. Many of the individuals I admire most are addicts in recovery. It isn't the person who uses and abuses you, it is the addiction. The best person becomes a nightmare when she becomes addicted. When she gets into recovery, she regains all her old strengths; and also, through the self-exploration with which she has had to engage to achieve her recovery, she has had the chance to gain a serenity to which the rest of us can only aspire. Until then, though, she will damage you as much as she damages herself.

Psychopaths

Very few psychopaths are like Hannibal Lecter. While many do get involved in crime at some point in their lives, they do so not on purpose, but because they don't know how not to.

The psychopath is disabled by an inability to understand the feelings of others or to learn from the consequences of his mistakes. If you don't cross him, he may well be very pleasant, but if you do, he will do whatever he needs to in order to get what he wants. When someone asks him why he punched his neighbor in the face, he is genuinely perplexed. 'Well, he was in my way. I wanted him out and he wouldn't go.' He doesn't understand why society is cross with him and he doesn't learn from the sanctions that society imposes.

The psychopath is under-aroused. That is, he feels deadened and it takes an awful lot to make him feel alive. Whereas you or I may get joy from a sunset, a song, or a child's gift, he can't feel anything unless it is extraordinary. Many such sensations are illegal, hence his tendency to fall foul of the law.

It isn't personal, but if you fall in his path he will hurt you, just because you are in his way. If you challenge him, you had better beware. He is very good at hurting and intimidating, as he has been doing it all his life. Unless you like a battle you will be in for a very tough time, and if you compete with him he will win, because while you've been busy being nice, he's been honing his skills at getting what he wants, whatever the cost. If you tend to road rage, you're playing Russian roulette because if you are unlucky enough to pick on a psychopath, you'll get hurt. Why did that chap cut you up at the junction back there? Just maybe because he is a psychopath and he felt like it.

Genuine full-blown psychopaths are quite rare, so don't lose sleep over it, but equally, picking fights with people you don't know is not a good idea.

Paranoid Possessors

Love, to my mind, is about giving; the welfare and happiness of your loved one are more important to you than your own. But not everyone sees it that way. To some, love means a need for the loved one, a craving for his attention and for having one's needs met. In such a relationship the paranoid possessor is at first very attentive, but over time becomes increasingly demanding. She clings, anxiously demanding proof of your love and fidelity. Any attempt to have a life of your own will be seen as evidence that you don't care. Your feelings become irrelevant in her quest to seek security and reassurance. She will increasingly question you about your whereabouts and if she learns that you have plans to do anything enjoyable that don't involve her, she will spike them. You may come to feel more like one of her possessions than her partner/spouse/friend, because that is really what you are. She can't give emotionally and she has to keep you where she can see you. She may give you lavish gifts, but these are really a way of binding you to her and she won't be slow to tell you how much you are in her debt (see below, 'Scorekeepers').

I use the label 'paranoid' in its colloquial sense here, that is, to imply that this person imagines wrongdoing behind her back. To psychiatrists the term is applied much more specifically to imply the presence of delusional psychotic illness. As I explain below, this type of person can develop psychotic illness, but it is unusual. What she does tend to exhibit is the phenomenon of projection. She will project her own unacceptable characteristics onto you and then attack you for them. So you may find her shouting, 'Why are you so angry and unreasonable all the time?', her face puce with rage as she spits fury in your direction, while you are at a loss to know how you could have been any more calm and rational, given the virulence of her attack.

At its most extreme, this picture becomes what psychiatrists call morbid, or delusional, jealousy. This syndrome can arise from various mental illnesses, in which case it will respond to treatment, or it may be a reflection of maladaptive personality development, in which case it will be more difficult to fix. This person will increasingly take her questioning of your fidelity to greater lengths.

Her inquisition will become ever more hostile. She will start producing spurious 'evidence' of your infidelity, such as marks on your clothing, with which she will confront you demanding a confession. This is a dangerous situation; among the psychiatric syndromes this one is most commonly associated with serious violence. If your partner conforms closely to this picture, seek professional advice. You may be in danger. Obviously, you need to use some judgement here. Because your wife questions you about your last business trip doesn't mean that she is about to turn into the crazed woman from *Fatal Attraction*.

The bottom line is that if you are feeling uncomfortably bound in your relationship, this is an issue that needs to be addressed, not ignored or complied with to keep the peace.

Scorekeepers

This individual uses giving as a weapon. He has a deep sense of injustice. He has given so much, but has anyone ever thanked him, or given him recognition for his sacrifice? Of course not. This is his life script and he is constantly looking for evidence to back it up. His gifts and hospitality will be over the top and when you don't reciprocate in kind, he will be offended. You have to dance to his tune or face his opprobrium, and you'd better be sure to give back at least as much as you're given, because he's keeping score. Very tiring and very dull, but very difficult to see coming or to extricate yourself from, as he seems so nice. It seems so mean to say no to someone who has given you so much. So you are enslaved.

Fundamentalists and Zealots

Whether it be a terrorist, a politician whose wish is to regulate everything that moves, or just your neighbor who demands that hedges must always be trimmed and cars must never touch the curb, these are undeniably pernicious people. Their certainty in their own rectitude makes people ill (and sometimes kills them). They take selected statutes or texts in total literal detail and allow for no other view than their own bigoted passion. If you are a giving, non-judgemental and accepting person you will probably have one of these people (and possibly more) in your life. While others will have told them to buzz off a long time ago, your ear is still there to be bent. If you fear leaving your front door, or visiting any place he frequents lest you get caught by this person, you have been afflicted by this disease.

You

OK, I've made this point before, but I'll make it again. If you are like most of my patients, your main attacker is you. The judgements that you make about yourself, the amount you expect of yourself and the criticism you heap on your own head when things go wrong are all much worse than the worst that can be done to you by others. You are a cruel and vicious person, but only to yourself. Strange, as you are so good to others.

Pernicious Places

Some environments are institutionally toxic. If you stay in them for too long, you lose sight of what is clear to others, but the truth is that these places make people sick. In organizations this process tends to evolve slowly at first, then gather pace and become more concrete later on. This happens because culture endures.

In a place populated by good people, with encouraging and enabling structures, the morale of those in it tends to be high. The word gets around and others want to work (or stay, or study, or visit, or whatever) there. The best people come and the quality rises further. A 'can do' culture exists in which those involved do more than what is expected of them and everyone supports everyone else. It takes quite a high level of incompetence for those in charge to mess this up, because the culture keeps the place going. But eventually, if management, or politicians, neglect it enough, push it too hard or strangle it in regulation and bureaucracy, even high-quality employees will become demotivated and morale will fall. People start doing only the minimum, become fearful, defensive and self-absorbed, and keep their head down, seeking to blame others as more and more goes wrong. The culture shifts to 'that's not my job'. Word gets around. Good people who have a choice don't want to work there. Quality falls.

If you are a backsliding shirker, this is the place for you. But if you are a diligent person who cares and tries to make things right, you are in danger. You can't change an institution. If you try too hard for too long, the place will slowly, passively, miserably grind you down until you get ill. Then you will be blamed for your lack of robustness. The blame game is played enthusiastically in these places, though not to enable any useful learning.

Some of you, having read this chapter, will be berating yourself: 'How could I have been so gullible as to let him do this to me? I'm such a fool. Why didn't I stand up to him ages ago? I should have seen what he is like.'

No, you shouldn't. You didn't know. It isn't your fault. In any case, life is about learning, not getting it right all the time. I've made plenty of mistakes in my life. I've let a few of the characters represented in this chapter hurt me too, but I banished them eventually, when I realized they were abusive, and I've learned my lessons. No doubt there are more to learn and more nasty people to bump into, among all the lovely ones I'm lucky enough to meet. You could probably add a few descriptions to my list of pernicious people. The key is to let experience be your teacher, and not to add to the damage these characters do by beating yourself up. Give yourself a break, but do have a think about the implications. I'll discuss them later.

One more thing. Toxic people can change if they really want to, and sometimes with help. But look at actions rather than words. Promises are cheap.

5

The Stress Illnesses

Physical Illnesses

As I mentioned in Chapter 1, we aren't designed for long periods of stress. Adrenaline gears us up very efficiently for a fight to the death with a sabre-tooth tiger, but it isn't well designed for three weeks of stress leading up to the year-end figures. There are a number of physical consequences to running your body at extra-hot for long periods, in the same way as if you ran a car at top revs all the time.

But the pains you are getting in your chest are not likely to be a heart attack. Much more probably they are the result of muscle tension. The risk of long-term over-arousal is long term, not now, so settle down. You're not going to die imminently. If you are concerned, see your doctor, but not if she just reassured you that you were physically fit last week when you had the same symptoms. Reassurance can be addictive; take it sensibly, not in excess.

This doesn't mean that symptoms caused by stress are all in the mind. Far from it. There is no division between mind and body. The physical effects that you suffer when you are under stress have a real physical basis, caused by the effects of adrenaline that I described earlier. So the muscles in your forehead really are in spasm when you have a headache; there really is inflammation in your stomach causing it to ache; the nerves in your hands and feet really are firing when you get pins and needles in your extremities. So if your doctor says that your symptoms are caused by stress, don't accuse him of telling you it's all in your mind – he isn't and it isn't.

The Cardiovascular System

Adrenaline is a short-term hormone. It isn't supposed to hang around for long, for the reasons I have given. If you live on adrenaline, your body assumes that the life-threatening danger for which the hormone is designed remains present. It responds by raising blood pressure, to get blood around the body. Some blood vessels, deep inside the body, constrict while those at the surface open up, to lose heat. Constriction of vessels to the kidney leads to production of another hormone, which increases blood pressure further; the kidney is pumping up the pressure in an attempt to preserve its blood supply, but if this state of affairs goes on for long, it sets up a vicious cycle of increasing blood pressure.

Meanwhile the adrenal glands, from which adrenaline is released, also produce more cortisol. This hormone increases the blood's tendency to coagulate, the purpose being to reduce bleeding if the body is injured in the attack it is anticipating. The problem is that this also leads to a tendency for blood to coagulate within the body, notably in the vessels supplying the heart and brain. This leads to an increased long-term risk of heart attacks (death of heart muscle when a branch of the coronary arteries becomes blocked) and strokes (interruption of blood supply to a part of the brain causing it to die).

The liver produces and releases more cholesterol and other fats; these are a good long-term supply of energy for muscles and other organs. The body assumes these will be needed to escape the persisting danger that it faces. But if this energy isn't used, the fats merely collect around the blood vessels and clog them up. In the vessels supplying the heart, this can further increase the risk of developing angina (pain from insufficient blood supply to the heart muscle) and heart attacks. The more exercise you take, the lower the risk, as these fats are used up to produce the energy you are using.

In the kidney, the deposited cholesterol can reduce blood supply, thus accelerating the production of the hormones causing raised blood pressure, adding to the vicious cycle. In the brain it can lead to strokes (death of part of the brain) through blockage of the blood vessels or through a vessel bursting under the weight of the increased blood pressure. In the muscles, particularly of the limbs, it can lead to pain on exertion and weakness, through restriction of blood supply at times when more is needed, during exercise (intermittent claudication).

The Gastro-Intestinal System

Under stress, the movement of the bowel increases. The body is trying to lose weight quickly, in order to run faster through jettisoning weight by evacuating the bowel. Stomach acid and bowel enzyme production is accelerated, in order to get more energy from food into the body quickly, so as to be able to run or fight. If this carries on for too long, the stomach becomes inflamed (gastritis) and can even become eroded, so that a hole is punched through the inner lining (ulcer). Acid may escape up the esophagus, the tube connecting the mouth with the stomach, leading to pain and inflammation (acid reflux, heartburn). If the stress endures, the muscles surrounding the bowel, having been overused for some time, may intermittently go into spasm and the bowel become inflamed, leading to painful and irregular bowel action, with diarrhea, constipation, or both at different times (irritable bowel syndrome).

The Immune System

Stress, as I have already mentioned, leads to the body producing more than is usual of the hormone cortisol. This has an anti-inflammatory action, allowing an animal to keep going for longer when under attack and to be less vulnerable to the effects of injury. The downside is that the immune system becomes less active as a result. If this carries on long term, the body becomes more prone to infections. We all know that we tend to get bugs when we are 'run down'.

Stress may also lead to a higher incidence of some cancers. Cancer cells appear in all of our bodies quite often. Mostly they are mopped up quickly by the immune system, but if it is compromised by chronic stress, the chance of some such cells slipping by is increased. There is also some evidence that, even if you have cancer, the level of stress you are suffering (of course, the disease is enough stress in itself) can influence the body's ability to fight off the disease, to survive it and to tolerate the necessary treatment.

The Peripheral Nervous System

Nerves become super-sensitive under the influence of adrenaline. This is necessary, in situations of life-threatening danger; you need your wits about you when a big cat is on your trail. But if you are sitting passively at home or the office, this has unfortunate consequences. Every physical sensation or symptom is magnified. Aches and pains that you would normally shrug off or ignore become intense and scary. Aha, scary – I know how to respond to that, says the body – more adrenaline! More super-sensitivity. More symptoms.

So your symptoms do have a physical basis. If you continue to be afflicted by stress, the number of symptoms affecting you can multiply, as can their severity. I once had a patient who at first couldn't believe that her symptoms were caused by stress, despite being thoroughly investigated and no other cause being found. After a while, I suggested that she list each new symptom as it arose, rather than chasing around getting more investigations. Eventually she accepted that she was probably suffering from stress. By that point, she had listed 198 symptoms.

There is no limit to the symptoms that stress can produce.

Motor nerves (the ones that connect the brain to the muscles, allowing movement) also become overactive, leading to the muscular problems listed below. So do autonomic nerves (the ones supplying the organs of which we are unaware, such as the bowel, heart and other internal organs), leading to the effects I have already described.

The Musculo-Skeletal System

Muscle tension is useful in short bursts for running or fighting. But if any muscle is in tension for too long it will go into spasm, particularly if it isn't designed for long-term use. Some muscles are designed for such extended action, such as the postural muscles, those made to hold us upright. Most of these are around the spine and legs. Other muscles, which tend to be around the shoulders, neck, jaw and arms, are not designed to hold you still but to move rapidly – to throw, tear, pull, push, bite and punch. These 'ballistic' muscles don't respond well to being held in tension for long periods, and spasm easily. When we are stressed, we tend to adopt 'defensive postures'. Our shoulders hunch, our arms are held close to our bodies, our fists ball, our heads are held forward, towards our chests, our teeth are clenched. Also, our facial muscles, designed for a range of expressions, are held in a tight grimace, with a furrowed brow. We are using ballistic muscles for posture. They don't work that way for long, though briefly they make you ready for a fight.

I know from personal experience about the effects of using ballistic muscles for posture. I suffer repetitive strain injury in my right hand, right shoulder and forehead. This came from many hours of sitting at my desk writing, with my head turned to my left towards my patient and looking (and being) concerned. I've dealt with this by using a fountain pen that I don't have to grip so tightly, shifting my seating position from time to time, avoiding leaning on my right elbow, and making funny faces from time to time between patients – not in response to anything they said, but to move my facial and forehead muscles. I also consciously relax my muscles and 'shake myself down' several times a day. It works.

Muscle tension is the easiest physical effect of stress to combat, but it takes consistent practice. Doing the relaxation exercise described later in this book (see page 69) on a regular basis will deal with the problem.

The Endocrine (Hormone) System

In the short term, as I have mentioned, stress leads to the production of adrenaline. If it continues for a long period, it also leads to an increase in cortisol levels. Cortisol is the body's long-term stress hormone. Raised levels have unfortunate consequences.

More fats circulate in the bloodstream and the liver also releases glucose into the blood. As a result, the pancreas, which is the organ that produces insulin, has to produce more of this hormone to keep blood glucose levels under control. In turn the body, and in particular the liver, can become resistant to the effects of insulin. If you are drinking more in response to the stress you are experiencing, exercising less because you are exhausted and so putting on weight, there is a triple whammy hitting the liver. The liver eventually responds by becoming almost completely unresponsive to insulin, failing to store sugar, which builds up in the blood and tissues. This is type 2 diabetes, the avoidable type, which develops due to an unhealthy lifestyle. This condition puts further strain on the heart. Another vicious cycle.

The Reproductive System

As everybody knows, stress messes up your sex life. Directly, this is through exhaustion and performance anxiety. Once you have failed on one occasion to get an erection, or to get aroused, or to reach orgasm, you fear it happening again. Fear is incompatible with sexual arousal, so the problem multiplies.

Indirectly, stress can also interfere with the production of sex hormones. Women may suffer irregularity of their periods or lose them altogether. Fertility reduces. Men further lose sexual interest and arousal, which is ironic, as in every other way, they are over-aroused. Diabetes and cardiovascular complications worsen the problem.

So extended stress can do you a lot of harm and may be life-threatening in the long term. It really is a life or death issue to bring the stress which is affecting you under control. But, let me say one more time, most stress-induced symptoms are not life-threatening. They are your friend, not your enemy: an indicator that you need to do something to change the way you are leading your life. Trust your doctor, who will tell you if your symptoms need specific physical investigation or treatment or not.

'Psychological' Illnesses

I put quotation marks in this heading because, as I have already said, the distinction between mind and body is a false one. The brain is an organ, albeit a very complex one. Once we understand the basis for a disorder of the brain we call it neurological; up to then we call it psychological. So while we realize that a brain tumor can cause aberrant behaviors, as yet we don't fully understand the neurology of obsessive-compulsive disorder, so this is classed as a psychiatric condition. In any case, excessive stress hurts your brain. Here are the brain disorders it can cause.

Anxiety (Generalized Anxiety Disorder) and Panic Disorder

Anxiety is fear in the absence of threat. As you will appreciate, there is a judgement involved here. One person's anxiety state is another's reasonable concern. Is it reasonable to be fearful of losing your job, of contracting a serious disease, of the tax inspector, of traveling by car? It all depends. If there are big layoffs looming, you smoke and are overweight, you have been a bit creative with your accounting, or you are traveling with a boy racer, then you had better be afraid. Move to a new job, lose weight, stop smoking, get advice from a good accountant, get out of the car and take public transportation. Whatever – your fear is telling you to take appropriate action.

But if you are fearful all the time, whatever the circumstances, you are suffering from an anxiety state. If you experience panic attacks frequently or occasionally, with palpitations, breathlessness, sweating, dizziness, feeling faint, shakiness and maybe tingling in your hands and feet, while feeling OK for much of the rest of the time, you suffer from panic disorder.

Either way, you are running too hot, at too high a level of arousal, right at the edge of the Yerke-Dodson curve (see Chapter 1). You have probably learned to be anxious from quite an early age. You try hard, push yourself and are self-critical. As likely as not, you tend to have a negative and catastrophic thinking style, seeing a disaster round every corner and assuming that if you aren't in control of everything all the time, things will go awry.

In either state, but especially in panic disorder, you will have developed the 'fear of fear'. You have your first panic attack. Though it is merely the fight-or-flight reaction (see Chapter 1) and totally harmless, it is a horribly frightening experience. You may feel as if you are going to die, because of the palpitations and breath-lessness. So the next time you approach a situation reminiscent of the one in which you had your first attack, you think: 'Oh no, I hope I don't have one of those horrible attacks again.' Your body reacts as it is designed to, with another fight-or-flight reaction and you develop another panic attack. And so your fears are confirmed. The next time you meet a situation which reminds you of the situation which reminded you of the situation in which the first attack occurred, it happens again, and so on and so on. Before you know it almost anything can trigger an attack.

Some people experience anxiety almost exclusively through physical symptoms (see above). This 'somatic anxiety' is not easy to treat as it feeds on itself and can be difficult to believe, making one disinclined to pursue and persevere with psychological treatments, because you are sure there is a terrible physical cause of your symptoms.

Either way, anxiety states and panic disorder can be among the most horrible conditions it is possible to suffer from. They can be totally disabling and often made worse by ill-informed 'friends' exhorting you to 'snap out of it' or 'pull yourself together'. In cases like this the strength of a person's opinions is often inversely proportional to their knowledge and wisdom. Ignore them, get treatment and look at the changes you need to make in your life. Getting rid of ignorant bullies from your list of friends may be a start.

Phobias (Phobic Anxiety Disorder)

A phobia is an unreasonable fear of a specific object or situation. This label is another that requires a judgement about reasonableness. A fear of spiders is probably not a phobia if you live in Australia where some are poisonous. When is a fear of heights a phobia? Most of us would feel fearful if we were perched a hundred feet up on a narrow ledge, though we could stand comfortably on the same platform a foot above the ground. It therefore depends on how unusual is the fear. Most important, how much does the fear impair our functioning? A fear of moon rock is of little relevance unless you are an astronaut, while agoraphobia, or a fear of being far from familiar surroundings (it isn't really a fear of open spaces), is potentially very disabling.

Some phobias aren't stress-related, but are there from a young age, or picked up from a parent. Many, though, are the result of a single traumatic experience or an extended period of suffering. So a person bullied by her boss may be terrified of going anywhere near her workplace well after the tormentor has moved to a different company. I see a lot of people who struggle to return to situations or places where they have been hurt, even though they know it won't happen again. This can be difficult to treat, though often not impossible. The reason is that such a sufferer has usually been away from the place or situation in which she suffered for quite some time before feeling well enough to return. All you have to do to develop a phobia is to have an experience causing trauma, then avoid the object of the trauma for long enough. Hence the adage that if you fall off a horse, you should get right back on again.

Another tricky one is social phobia, because the experience that has caused it often occurs at quite a young age. It feeds on itself somewhat, because the more you avoid social situations, the less skilled you become at handling them. This means you get fewer positive experiences when you do try to engage in such situations, and often a lot of embarrassment. Self-conscious self-criticism is at the root of this. People who can allow themselves to fail without berating themselves don't develop social phobia.

The other commonly disabling condition is claustrophobia. It can be difficult to trace the traumatic events that start this phobia. It tends to spread to an increasing number of situations, all having in common the inability to make quick escape at will. So elevators, airplanes, restaurants (with people who wouldn't understand if you rushed out), theaters and cinemas are often involved.

Whatever the phobic object or situation, the longer it is avoided, the worse it gets. On the other hand, any stress makes phobic anxiety, like generalized anxiety, worse. So pushing someone with a phobia too hard can make the phobia worse, by re-traumatization. Best seek advice.

Obsessive-Compulsive Disorder

I don't know for certain why some people manifest their over-arousal by becoming generally anxious, while others develop obsessive-compulsive disorder (OCD). It has something to do with personality traits, but I find that some of my OCD patients don't have obsessional personalities at all; that is, they aren't generally perfectionist, caught up with detail, inflexible or intolerant of change.

In any case, OCD is another manifestation of anxiety, caused by the brain's tendency to organize things into patterns. If you lie on the ground on a summer's day and look up at the clouds, you will, after a while, start seeing patterns in them: a coastal outline here, a face or a running animal there. This is because the brain is designed to see patterns in things, even when there is none present. For some, their anxiety gets organized in this way. Their over-arousal is made meaningful by the appearance of a set of distressing repetitive thoughts (obsessions) or actions (compulsions). Obsessions and compulsions have in common that they are repetitive, are generated by anxiety, feel alien and nonsensical to the person affected by them, are resisted, but eventually given in to when the resistance is overwhelmed by mounting anxiety. This leads to brief relief of anxiety after they are performed, only for the anxiety to return in force after a little while.

Obsessional thoughts are often 'magical', such as: 'If I don't think this rhyme every night, something awful will happen to my kids.' The sufferer is tormented by fear: 'What if something bad happens?' This type of fear is illustrated in the TV series *Lost* in which people trapped on a desert island find a computer and instructions that say they must enter a code every two hours to avoid an unnamed catastrophe. It's almost certainly nonsense as it doesn't make sense, but what if it's true? So they enter the code every two hours, day and night, just in case.

The second type of obsessional thoughts are often shocking. These cause immense distress to the sufferer. So a loving father may suddenly fear that he might murder his family in their beds, or a devoutly religious woman may suddenly start getting pornographic images of a man's genitals in her mind. These types of obsessional thoughts are the most shocking thoughts *for you* that your brain can dream up. You won't act on them as that isn't what they are about. What they tell us is about your values; what you find most shocking. But the sufferer is deeply ashamed of having the thoughts and often feels that they indicate that he is evil or perverted. He is very alone with his distress, as he can't share his thoughts with anyone, with good reason. Most people wouldn't understand.

The third type of obsessional thought is obsessional doubting, where a person spends most of his time agonizing over whether to make choice A or choice B. If you tell him to choose A he will choose B. Then he regrets his choice and switches to A, only to feel he shouldn't have switched and so returns to B, and so on ad infinitum. So a husband has an affair and tells his mistress that he will leave his wife to be with her; but then he has doubts and breaks off the affair, telling his wife that the dalliance is over. Then he regrets cutting off his chance of greater happiness and goes back to his mistress, only to realize what he is losing and returning to his wife; and so on and so on. It's remarkable how long the spouses and partners of these doubters put up with this torment, but of course eventually they tire of it and the doubter loses both.

Compulsive actions may have a surface validity, but become nonsensical through repetition. So a woman may have to wash her hands ten times after using the toilet and twice after touching any object. She may have to check that the gas is turned off seven times after leaving the kitchen last thing at night. Or there may be no sense in the repeated actions, such as a motorist retracing his route every time he has driven somewhere, just in case he may have knocked down a pedestrian without noticing during his journey. Either way, the compulsive actions reflect underlying obsessional thoughts and the compulsions can take over a person's life. Eventually the obsessive compulsive may become confined to one room, having no time for anything other than his compulsions.

Post-Traumatic Stress Disorder (PTSD)

This is a specific form of stress-related illness that occurs after a person has experienced a highly traumatic event. It was first studied in the First World War when it was referred to as shell shock. Unfortunately, the army was not inclined to admit that these men were ill, preferring to view them as cowards, so many of those affected faced the firing squad. In the Second World War it was called battle fatigue. This time there was more willingness to understand and after the war asylums were opened where sufferers were treated and the condition studied. In recent years survivors of terrorist attacks and hostage ordeals have provided plenty of opportunity for further research.

Nowadays the commonest cause of PTSD in patients referred to me is road traffic accidents.

PTSD typically occurs when a person believes, if only for a moment in anticipation of the impact, that she will die or be terribly injured; or in witnessing a traumatic event, the person believes that a loved one is suffering, will suffer terribly, or will die. It tends to happen more to people who are affected by stress and its illnesses anyway, but it can happen to anyone, given trauma which is experienced as terribly disturbing.

The symptoms emerge hours to some weeks after the event. The central one is *flashbacks*: vivid and intrusive memories of the event. These may be visual, like a film clip of the car approaching; auditory, like a tape of the sound of crunching metal; olfactory, such as the smell of burning fuel after the impact; tactile, such as pain from an injured limb; or gustatory, such as the taste of blood, for instance following being hit in the face by the steering wheel. In any case, these flashbacks cause great distress.

Together with flashbacks, a variety of other symptoms can be developed, including some, but usually not all of the following: a feeling of emotional *numbness*; *withdrawal* from social situations; *irritability*; *jumpiness* or a tendency to startle easily; *inability to relate* normally to family and friends; *loss of interest* in everyday things; *anxiety*; *depression*; and *avoidance of cues* that remind her of the event. She may avoid driving or being a passenger in a car, make long detours to avoid the scene of the accident, or be unable to watch anything on TV involving injury or death.

The flashbacks, hyper-arousal and withdrawal may render her totally unable to lead her life and this may go on for a long time if untreated. Sadly, the trauma of the event is sometimes surpassed by the losses that can follow a long period of symptoms: job, relationships, interests and self-esteem. However, in far more cases, the symptoms gradually fade over time, whether treated or not.

Depressive Illness (Major Depression, or Depressive Episode)

This is the subject of my book *Overcoming Depression: The Curse of the Strong* (also published by Westminster John Knox Press). If you suffer from this horrid illness, I suggest you read it. I will only outline a few points from the book here:

- Most cases of depressive illness are caused by a combination of too much stress and trying too hard to overcome the stress; that is, trying to achieve the unachievable.
- It is a physical, not a mental illness.
- It is not the same as 'feeling depressed'.
- You don't know how terrible it is unless you have had it yourself.
- You can't 'pull yourself out of it'.
- It happens to the best people; that is, people who are strong, reliable, diligent, responsible, with a strong conscience, undemanding of others but very demanding of themselves, sensitive and with a self-esteem that isn't difficult to dent.
- The symptoms include feeling worst in the morning and gradually better as the day goes on. Others comprise a list of 'loss ofs': loss of sleep and appetite (although occasionally these are increased instead), energy, enthusiasm, concentration, memory, confidence, self-esteem, sex drive, drive, enjoyment, patience, feelings, optimism – in fact, loss of almost everything.
- It tends to get better sooner or later, but keeps coming back unless you make changes in the way you think and operate (the opposite side to this coin is that you can usually avoid recurrence by making changes in your life).
- It gets better quicker if you rest, take active treatment, avoid folk remedies, pace yourself slowly in recovery and challenge prejudices about it such as: 'It is shameful'; 'It is a weakness'; 'I can defeat it by trying harder'; 'Antidepressants do you harm'. Avoid amateur advice ('I saw in *TIME* magazine/I was told by Mrs. Smith from down the street/I read on the internet – that taking infusions of boiled atlas beetle dung every three hours is natural and much better than Prozac'). Ask your doctor to help you, and if he/she doesn't, find one who will. Don't rely on non-medical sources in making your decisions on treatment. After all, I wouldn't go to my butcher for legal advice.

Addictions

An addiction is any set of actions that you employ to stop yourself from experiencing unpleasant feelings, which then becomes out of control. It is you treating yourself for the effects of stress without dealing with the root causes. It is doomed to failure, for the reasons that I gave in Chapter 2 (under 'Alcohol and Other Drugs'). In addiction, the symptoms you take alcohol or other substances to combat escalate over time. The same applies for all addictive drugs, whether they be tranquillizers, sleeping tablets or heroin. All these substances work at first, but over time they make the problem that they were taken to fix much worse. Some can also lead to serious physical illness. I won't go into those here.

Addiction isn't just about drugs, though. Whatever you do to make your feelings go away can become an addiction if it gets out of control. This may be spending money on things you don't need, comfort eating, engaging compulsively in unwise relationships because of dependence on people or sex, gambling, or just habitually running away from uncomfortable feelings by whatever means are at hand.

All of these addictive behaviors, and many more, can take over your life and destroy it if you don't stop. The priority is dealing with the addiction first, then the underlying issues later. It has to be this way round, but more of that later.

Psychotic Illnesses

Occasionally stress can lead to a complete breakdown in the way the brain functions. There is, incidentally, no such thing as a 'nervous breakdown'. As far as I can make out, it is a term some people (but not psychiatrists) use to refer to an episode of illness severe enough to require admission to hospital, but it doesn't have any real meaning.

Stress-induced psychotic episodes may arise out of severe depression, result from drug or alcohol use, or just come out of nowhere in someone who is very stressed. They may involve clearly depressed or elated moods or fluctuations between the two. They often involve *delusions*: fixed false beliefs not explainable in terms of the person's culture. For example, it may not be delusional for people from some parts of Africa to believe that they are bewitched. It isn't necessarily delusional to feel that people are talking about you, but it could be if this belief resists all rational argument and evidence over an extended period. The beliefs are often persecutory in nature, with the person believing he is under attack or surveillance. If he is depressed, he feels that the persecution is just punishment because of his badness or failures.

There may be *hallucinations*, that is, perceptions in the absence of any object. These can be visual (seeing things when there is nothing there), auditory (such as hearing voices when nobody is speaking) or indeed may involve any of the senses. Misinterpreting a sensation is not a hallucination; it is an illusion and is not a sign of psychotic illness. An example would be seeing a coin on the floor and thinking it is a mouse. In contrast, hallucinations usually indicate psychotic illness, or the presence of a physical illness. An exception is hallucinations occurring just as you are going to sleep, when you are very drowsy, or when you are just waking up. They can happen to anyone who is stressed. I know when I'm working too hard because I occasionally get a disturbing experience just as I'm dropping off to sleep. I hear a sound, as clear as day, of a hundred metal trash cans being dropped off of a fire escape onto the street below. Alarming though this is for me (and my wife), it doesn't mean I'm psychotic.

Sometimes *thought disorder*, or a disruption of the pattern of thinking, makes it impossible for a person to follow his train of thought or understand what he is talking about. This isn't referring to the habit of so many of us to be, at times, illogical, but reflects a complete disruption of the person's cognitive processes, such as: 'You for three I have brown down thing bad.' Yes, I know, I tend to talk a bit like that when I'm very tired too, but the pattern of thought disorder is unmistakable if you spend a few minutes with a person exhibiting it.

The actions of a person with psychotic illness may be organized, if she is acting on her delusions, or bizarre and disorganized. She may have other symptoms too, such as feeling that she can hear the thoughts of others or that they can hear hers; that thoughts are put into her head, or that parts of her body are not under her control. These symptoms, though, are more common in schizophrenia, which is not a stress-induced illness (though sufferers are very sensitive to stress) and which is beyond the scope of this book.

Psychotic illness needs urgent treatment. The longer someone is ill, the more difficult it is successfully to treat her illness. Treated promptly, a stress-induced psychotic episode, particularly a first one, can often respond quickly. If the causes of the underlying stress are dealt with too, people with psychotic illness, like the victims of other stress-induced illnesses, can then stay well.

6

Treatments Which Help You Get Better

Whichever of the illnesses that stress can cause has afflicted you, the bottom line is the same. You've been running too hot for too long. This has partly been because of your circumstances, but also because of you. Life's jerks have been grinding you down, but only because you let them. I'll come to what to do with them later, but for now we need 'urgent inaction'. You're a juggernaut, piling onwards regardless of how much damage it has done you. Now you're ill. So, first of all, STOP.

Stop doing what you've been doing. If work, in part or in whole, has made you ill, go to the doctor and take sick leave. If you've been exhausting yourself meeting the demands of others, get yourself diagnosed and then tell them that you're ill. You can't do what you always have done for them, for now at least. If you got ill chasing personal goals, you have to pause for a while. Like an athlete who develops an injury through training too hard, you need to rest to give your injury time to heal. Whichever of the ailments listed in Chapter 5 you have developed, you have a real illness with a physical basis. It isn't in your mind, and you can't pull yourself out of it by effort or determination. The harder you try, the worse it will get.

If you feel as if you're on the edge of a precipice, it's because you are – so pull back. It's in everyone's interests for you to do so, even if those around you (boss, spouse, friends, kids) moan about it now. They don't understand about stress-related illness and there's no reason why they should; they've never experienced it. If you stop driving yourself further into the mire right now, at least things won't get worse, and if you give yourself time to rest you will start to heal. Then some specific treatments can help you to recover.

Once that's been achieved we can get to the most rewarding part:

staying well. But unless you stop what made you ill in the first place right now, nothing else will work. Remember, it's not the stress that made you ill, it was you trying to do the undoable. So I say again – STOP.

Don't read any further until you've done this, because none of the rest of this book will work until you have brought yourself to a halt. If you don't know how to do so, see your doctor, find a counselor or talk to a wise friend – not one who will tell you to pull yourself together, but one who has already recognized that things aren't right with you. Get him or her to read this chapter up to here. Then discuss how, in your particular circumstances, you can stop.

You won't be able to sit in a chair and just do nothing; you're too agitated for that. Do whatever is easy, but nothing that is challenging or takes effort. The ideal is an undiluted diet of Australian soap operas. Television of that sort can stop you ruminating without requiring any real thought or concentration. If that doesn't work for you, do whatever you find easy. I love watching television; it lets my brain turn to putty for a while and I find that a relief. But if what lets you switch off is stamp collecting, gardening or juggling with coconuts, so be it. So long as it allows you to rest. Of course, it won't work completely, as you're too stressed to be able to feel rested, but if it allows you to feel blank, in neutral, not so tormented, it'll do. Now bookmark this page and don't continue until you have come to rest.

OK, now that you've stopped spinning like a top, I've got your attention. I know you're not feeling any better yet; you're probably feeling worse, if anything. That's not surprising, as you don't realize how poorly you are doing until you stop to feel it. But you've done the hardest part. You've stopped the juggernaut. Now the treatments can work.

Here are some of the standard treatments that are used for stress-induced conditions. Get yourself treated, putting aside any prejudices you may have about any of these methods. Then we can get on to how you can stay well, through acting on the knowledge that you have gained from the earlier chapters of this book.

The Therapies

Relaxation Training

The relaxation exercise here is the same as in my *Overcoming Depression* book, so some readers may be familiar with it already.

The best way to combat stress is to learn and become expert at a relaxation exercise. There are many variations on this theme and the important thing is to find the one that works best for you. A number of relaxation tapes are commercially available and many people find it easiest to learn the techniques by listening to one of these. Others get benefit from yoga techniques learned in a group setting. Some find that following a written set of instructions is more helpful, allowing them to do the exercise at their own pace with their own mental imagery. What follows is just one example of such a technique, which many of my patients have found helpful.

Whichever way you choose, the essential point is that it needs a lot of practice. Though a few people pick it up very quickly, for the majority relaxation techniques do not work at all to start with. Some people even feel worse at the beginning, because doing anything and then failing tends to make you feel tense.

Persevere, because when you really master the technique you will find that it changes your life, allowing you to deal with situations that previously you could not have coped with at all. The people who get benefit from relaxation exercises are those who put them at the top of their list of priorities and practice for at least half an hour every day, come hell or high water. Looking back, I did relaxation exercises every day for about three years, not because I'm unusually anxious, but because I think that everybody can benefit from them. It took about a month of daily practice for the exercise to be any use at all. It took me at least three months before I was able to use it before an exam, because the most difficult time to do a relaxation exercise effectively is when you most need it, at times of high stress. After two to three years I got to the stage of no longer needing the exercise because I could switch on a relaxed state like a light when necessary. I can tell you that gaining this ability is worth all the time and effort.

A Relaxation Exercise (See cartoon on page 70.)

Spend 15–20 minutes on this exercise.

1 Find a suitable place to relax. A bed or an easy chair is ideal, but anywhere will do, preferably quiet and private. If your seat in the office or a house full of children is all there is, it can still be done.
2 Try to clear your mind of thoughts as far as you can.
3 Take three very slow, very deep breaths (10–15 seconds to breathe in and out once).
4 Imagine a neutral figure. An example might be the number 1. Don't choose any object or figure with an emotional signifi- cance, such as a ring or a person, for example. Let it fill your mind. See it in your mind's eye, give it a color, try to see it in 3- D and repeat it to yourself, under your breath, many times over. Continue until it fills your mind.
5 Slowly change to imagine yourself in a quiet, peaceful and pleasurable place or situation. This may be a favorite place or situation, or a pleasant scene from your past. Be there, and notice all the feelings, in each sense. See it, feel it, hear it and smell it. Spend some time there.
6 Slowly change to be aware of your body. Notice any tension in your body. Take each group of muscles in turn. Tense, then relax them two or three times each. Include fingers, hands, arms, shoulders, neck, face, chest, tummy, buttocks, thighs, legs, feet and toes. Be aware of the feeling of relaxation. When complete, spend some time in this relaxed state.
7 Slowly get up and go about your business.

Don't hurry this procedure and remember to practice. It will work.

Counseling and Supportive Psychotherapy

These are psychotherapies designed to be short term in nature which focus on your current problems. They don't seek to explore beyond the issues at hand. Rather than looking past your mental defenses, they seek to help you to build and strengthen them. The emphasis is on support, sharing problems and finding coping strat- egies, employing listening, empathy, common sense and wisdom rather than any more specific model as the tools of treatment. Most

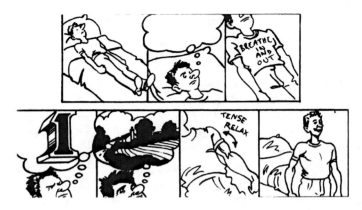

therapists you can find at your local counseling center will have the skills to carry out these forms of therapy, or you can search the web to find a therapist in your area. One way or another, you should be able to get some counseling, if that is what you need. Start by talking to your doctor.

Behavioral Psychotherapy

This treatment works on conditioning principles and is used to treat phobic anxiety states and OCD. Nowadays it is often combined with CBT techniques (see below).

If you have a phobia, the first thing the therapist will do is to teach you a relaxation technique (see page 69). Next you will be asked to draw up a list of feared situations, in ascending order. For example, if you have a phobia of spiders, at the bottom of your hierarchy might be looking at a picture of a small spider; slightly higher would be watching a video of a spider; higher still, looking at a spider in a sealed glass box thru the other side of a window; and at the top may be having spiders crawling over your body. The therapist will have you design as many rungs as possible to this ladder, then you will start at the bottom and deal with each situation, only going on to the next rung when you are pretty comfortable with the last one. In this way none of the steps should feel big or very scary, as you will have done something nearly at that level already.

This process, called *systematic desensitization*, is performed while using the relaxation technique, on the principle of *reciprocal inhibition*, meaning that you can't be both anxious and relaxed at the same time. By performing an anxiety-provoking action having pre-treated yourself with a relaxation exercise, you will experience it less fearfully. Because the experience is not negative, your brain is reconditioned not to fear the situation, so the next time you approach it, you won't fear it in the way you did. Eventually if the therapy is successful, in small steps, you will lose your phobia completely.

In OCD a similar principle is used, gradually and methodically reducing the frequency of your compulsive actions. Obsessional thoughts are a bit more difficult to treat in this way and usually require the addition of CBT.

Cognitive-Behavioral Therapy (CBT)

This is the therapy most often used nowadays to treat most stress-related illnesses, because it works (it has a lot of evidence behind it) and it tends to do so quickly (unlike exploratory/psychodynamic/analytical therapy). This makes it both practical and affordable; important since many health insurance programs do not sufficiently cover mental health services. Many counseling centers and other providers offer services on a sliding payment scale, depending on your income, so it is worth pursuing even if you think you cannot afford it.

The 'cognitive' part refers to your thoughts and the 'behavioral' part to your actions. The therapist will look for the negative thinking patterns that underpin your experiences of stress and then dig further for the deeply held underlying assumptions that underpin them. A negative thought may be: 'I will do badly in the presentation I have to do tomorrow.' The underlying assumptions may be: 'I will always be found wanting' and 'If I ever get optimistic, fate will play a trick on me'. If you habitually think this way, you will suffer from stress, whatever you do. It isn't your fault, because you've been taught to expect the worst from an early age, by bitter experience. But until you learn to think realistically, to unlearn the faulty learning, to reprogram the old computer that is your brain, you won't be consistently happy and will be prone to stress-related illness.

CBT does this by taking the thoughts and assumptions that plague you and challenging them in a very structured way. Through taking your experiences as they happen, looking at how the emotions they lead to reflect your habitual thinking errors and then challenging them, the therapist will teach you to think realistically, therefore experiencing the world as a less threatening place in which you have more control and influence than you realized. You will be asked to record events, thoughts, emotions and mood and to see for yourself how challenging negative thinking patterns makes you feel better. Once it has worked, you will be able to identify your thinking errors promptly on the spot and to change them. You will become your own traveling therapist.

I CBT myself every day. It works. There are plenty of opportunities to feel bad in my job. I've learned to deal with these realistically, which allows me to absorb the ups and downs thrown me by my patients without being affected too much. This keeps me effective and well. I can't recommend CBT highly enough, if you can find a good therapist.

Exploratory (Psychodynamic) Psychotherapy

In years past a lot of stress-related illness was treated with psychoanalysis. It is used much less today. This therapy often involved seeing a therapist several times a week and was a very thorough exploration of everything in the patient's life and psyche, sometimes taking years to be completed. We mostly don't have the time or resources for this nowadays, life being as rushed as it is. But if your problems originate very clearly from early on in your life and fail to respond to briefer interventions, you may be recommended this form of therapy, in a somewhat more streamlined form. This is called brief focal therapy, which summarizes it pretty well, as it focuses primarily on the aspects of your experience and current mental functioning that underpin your problems.

Psychodynamic therapists tend to be less active and directive than cognitive therapists. They see their role as helping you to find your own recovery rather than delivering it to your door. Metaphorically, if your mind is a dark forest and you are lost in the middle of it, a cognitive therapist will lead you out by the shortest route, while the psychodynamic therapist will merely suggest some interesting directions to take, holding your hand as you start to walk in that direction and pointing out landmarks along the way.

CBT gets you out quicker, but exploratory therapy gives you a more thorough understanding of the forest.

The tools used include *working through*; that is, looking at and re-experiencing events and their attendant feelings. The key to this is repetition. The therapist will take you over the same ground time and again, looking at it from up and down and this way and that. Thus the bottled-up feelings are released and understood. *Transference* refers to the powerful feelings that the client will tend to develop towards his therapist, which tend to reflect feelings that have been engendered in him by other pivotal people in his life. These can then be looked at, explored and worked through, freeing him from the vulnerability that he has to situations and people that resurrect these feelings. This is the phenomenon of *resonance*: the way in which any experience that isn't worked through at the time is stored up and then added to any experience in the future that your mind links to it, because they are either similar or symbolically similar to each other. I've illustrated this with an example on page 37.

From your point of view, what is needed is honesty and openness with your therapist and avoidance of *acting out*. This is the opposite of talking in (therapy). For example, if you have problems with anger which lead you to be referred to a therapist, you could road rage on your way to the session, driving on the bumper of the car in front, shouting, beeping your horn, making rude gestures and generally being a pest. By the time you get to your session, your anger will have dissipated and there will be nothing real to work on, except in theory. If, on the other hand, you don't road rage, you'll arrive at your session with green smoke pouring out of your ears owing to the silliness of your fellow road users. Now, there is real live emotion, in the session, fuel for the therapy to work on.

Talk in; don't act out. *Insight* into your issues, their origins and the *defense mechanisms* which you have used to get by, but which now are harming you, are also important elements of this type of therapy, but it is not an end in itself. Understanding your issues doesn't make them go away unless you have also worked them through.

While the evidence for the effectiveness of this type of therapy for stress-related conditions isn't as strong as that for CBT, it can be a powerful tool for change in some.

Cognitive-Analytical Therapy (CAT)

This therapy does pretty much what the name says. It incorporates the principles of CBT, while also involving a degree of appropriate exploration and analysis of mental mechanisms. It's more structured than psychodynamic therapy, but arguably less directive and formulaic than CBT. It's a fairly new therapy, so few therapists, if they are absolutely honest, will claim to be experts in it yet. We are gaining experience as we go. It's in its early days, but CAT seems to work well for those whose negative thinking patterns clearly need CBT, but who also have issues and experiences in their past and present which need working through.

Problem-Solving

Again, if you've read my *Overcoming Depression* book, you will be familiar with this technique.

The trouble with problems is that they don't come one at a time but, like buses, in batches. When you're in one of these spells, the weight of problems seems so overwhelming that you don't know where to start. The whole thing seems like a gigantic mess. You can't tolerate things being out of control, so you try to deal with everything at once, resulting only in chasing your tail and becoming increasingly frustrated and overheated. You get irritable with your spouse, thus losing her support and understanding. Now you have yet another problem to deal with, because you've tried to do too much at once.

The principle of problem-solving is simple: take a set of problems or one big problem and split it up into smaller pieces. Let's take an example. You are in a financial mess. The problem is too big to manage as a whole, so split it up:

1 I'm above my overdraft limit at the bank.
2 My creditors are getting insistent.
3 I'm spending beyond my means.
4 My debtors aren't paying up.
5 The mortgage rate has gone up.
6 The car is on its last legs.
7 Christmas is just around the corner.

Now you have a set of smaller and more manageable problems to sort out. Take each one in turn and 'brainstorm' some possible actions. This means including all your ideas on what to do, the apparently bad ones as well as the obviously sensible ones. For example, for problem 1 a possible list might be:

a Ask the bank to extend my overdraft limit.
b Explain that the problem is largely of cash flow, that I am addressing it, and it should only be temporary.
c Take out a short-term loan.
d Borrow from friends/relatives.
e Cut out items of expenditure (see problem 3).
f Ignore it.
g Do more overtime.
h Move to a new house.
i Change jobs.

Now think each option through and reject those that don't work. Talk it through with someone, if it helps.

Do this process for each of the points that you originally listed. Several of the action points will recur. Gather them together and then put them in a list of priority and act on them one at a time. Check them off as you do each one. The process of working through the list is very satisfying and allows you to feel that you are doing everything that can be done to improve the situation.

Of course, following this structure for problems does not make them go away, but it does give you more control over them. Stress tends to happen when you feel that you have lost control over your life. You can't get the control back through effort alone. You need to act strategically, with organization and patience. Don't try to make it all happen at once.

Mindfulness

This technique is in its infancy, at least in the UK. It was developed in the USA over 20 years ago, but has only taken off in the UK in the last few years. This technique is usually taught in groups, but doesn't tend to require a lot of interaction, which makes it easy to tolerate for those who don't like baring their souls in front of strangers. It was developed as a relapse prevention technique for people who had recurrent episodes of depression, though nowadays it is used for all sorts of stress-related conditions and for those who are still ill as well as those who are recovered.

Mindfulness training is based on the observation that once a person has recovered from an episode of depression or other stress-related illness, a fairly small degree of depressed mood can trigger a large amount of negative thoughts, such as: 'My recovery has stalled, I'm back to square one, I'll never get better, I'm a failure', and so on. This leads to more depressed mood and so a vicious cycle is set up in which the person's reaction is way out of proportion to the normal fluctuations of mood that triggered it. The more she searches for an answer or remedy for this spiral, the more her ruminations drag her down. This out-of-proportion response is very powerful and traumatic. As a result, the brain forms a strong association between the low mood and the negative thoughts that followed. So next time your mood is low, as it is bound to be sometimes (quite often in the early stages of recovery from stress-related illnesses), the negative thoughts and the whole vicious cycle will automatically start up again. If this carries on for long enough, relapse can be the result.

Mindfulness-based cognitive therapy (MBCT) helps you to stay in the present moment and to be aware of what is going on in your mind and body, and why. If you can recognize when your mood is going down without panicking or battling with it, but allow the changes in mood and the associated thoughts to happen, observing them and noting that they pass, you will prevent the vicious cycle from starting. This ability to be aware of yourself in the present also helps you to ruminate less about the past and worry less about the future. Not only is rumination and worry stressful, it's also useless. Nobody learned anything useful by going over and over past failures or worrying about the future. As I mentioned before, most of the bad things that happen in life fall out of a clear blue sky, while the things you spend days worrying over tend not to happen.

There is quite good evidence for the effectiveness of MBCT, especially in treating anxiety states and preventing relapse of depression, and an increasing number of therapists are using it. Hopefully, more MBCT groups will become available over the next few years, as it is a very cost-effective strategy.

Eye Movement Desensitization and Reprocessing (EMDR)

This is a type of therapy mainly used to treat PTSD, though it is now starting to be used to treat other stress-related conditions as well. I must say that at first EMDR smacked to me a bit of water-divining and tarot cards. I was wrong. It has now gained a powerful evidence base and definitely works for some people suffering from the effects of recent or past trauma.

The technique was discovered by the chance observation of an American psychologist, Francine Shapiro. She had experienced an upsetting incident some time before and was now suffering distressing thoughts about it, causing her to re-experience the event on a daily basis. Then one sunny day, she was walking through a park, and light from the sun was flickering in her eyes through the trees. All of a sudden her thoughts and the accompanying distress disappeared. She also noticed that when she brought the thoughts back to mind, they were not as upsetting or valid as before. She realized that the thoughts changed without conscious effort, and on paying close attention while thinking the thoughts, that her eyes were moving spontaneously and rapidly in an upward diagonal direction. She then set about investigating what it was that was responsible for the beneficial effect. Eventually it transpired that it wasn't the light, its pattern, its intensity or color that was important, but the particular eye movements.

EMDR therapists get you to move your eyes by following an object, while remembering the traumatic events; then noticing what is going on in your mind and with your feelings; and after a while reporting what you have noticed by way of a change in thoughts, feelings and images. They seek to reframe the event – helping you to see that it was in the past and doesn't directly affect the present – while utilizing the eye movements. Thus the emotional response and the memory of the events are disconnected, allowing you to consign the events to history and gain freedom from the emotions and associated symptoms which had previously dominated your attention.

EMDR is another treatment that has strong claims to cost-effectiveness, at least in some people with PTSD.

Drug Treatments

Medications in psychiatry have received a bad press in recent years. Given the dire quality of reporting of scientific matters in parts of the world's media, a true or balanced picture has often been obscured. As a journalist patient told me a while ago: 'We're not much bothered by the truth, so long as it's a good story.'

Sadly this fixation on sensationalism has led to many a patient who could have benefited greatly from timely drug treatment refusing it, and as a result recovery has been delayed needlessly, sometimes for years. It's not that pills are the answer to stress or its illnesses, any more than cardiac massage and the kiss of life are the answer to heart disease. But the best cardiological treatments are of no use if the first aid isn't administered when the patient has his cardiac arrest. Likewise, CBT doesn't work if your depression is so severe that your distorted perception renders you unreachable, or if you are in such a state of panic that you can't concentrate enough to take anything in. Medications are only first aid, but are nonetheless sometimes crucial. Don't refuse them on principle, but equally, don't accept them as the sole treatment of your stress-related illness. They may buy you time for the therapy to work and then for you to make the changes in your life that you need to make to stay well.

Antidepressants

These drugs are widely used, as you would expect, in the treatment of depression, but some of them also have an anxiety-reducing effect. There are several types, each acting in a different way. What they have in common is that they work in quite a subtle way on transmitter chemicals, which are substances released by nerve endings in the limbic system. This is a circuit made up of nerve fibers linking several different parts of the brain. Impulses have to cross a gap to get from one nerve to the next; this is achieved by an impulse reaching the end of one nerve causing the release of transmitter chemicals. These cross the gap to reach the next nerve fiber, at which point an impulse is set up that travels along that fiber, and so on. In depressive illness the levels of these chemicals plummets and so the circuit grinds to a halt, causing you to come to a halt too, as well as all the horrid symptoms of depression.

It isn't a metaphor to say that depressive illness is a blown fuse; the limbic system is a fuse and it's designed to blow if you are under too much pressure for too long. Antidepressants mend the fuse by replacing the lost chemicals, allowing the limbic circuit to run normally again. If you keep them going for long enough (at least six months from recovery for a first major depressive episode), the limbic system heals, allowing you gradually to withdraw the medication without the symptoms coming back. But of course, if you keep putting 18 amps through a 13 amp fuse it will keep blowing, so unless you change the way you think and operate, the depression will keep coming back. Then again, if you don't overload the fuse, it won't blow, so you can stay well if you make the right moves.

The way in which antidepressants help to control anxiety is more complex and, to be honest, we don't fully understand it yet. What we do know is that two mechanisms are involved. The first is that any antidepressant that has sedative actions will reduce arousal and so may help to reduce anxiety and stress-related conditions of all kinds. These include most tricyclic antidepressants (one of the older categories of drugs, around since the late 1950s), phenelzine, one of the MAOIs (monoamine oxidase inhibitors, the other older category of drugs) and mirtazapine (a more modern drug).

The second way in which antidepressants can reduce anxiety is through acting on the serotonin system. Serotonin is one of the transmitter chemicals in the limbic system and has a role, as yet not fully understood, in controlling anxiety levels. The SSRIs (selective serotonin reuptake inhibitors, drugs acting specifically on the serotonin system) often increase anxiety levels for the first one to two weeks, then lower it thereafter. This effect seems to be well maintained for as long as you take the medication, unlike addictive drugs, which lose their effect over time.

The problem is that if you take a pill to deal with anxiety, you may tend not to deal with the issues underpinning it. While I strongly advocate the use of antidepressants to treat depressive illness, I don't tend to use them much for people with anxiety. Someone physically ill with a clinical depressive illness will have grossly distorted perception as one of the symptoms of the condition. How can such a person benefit from any of the therapies outlined above? It's a rhetorical question; they can't, as all of these therapies require you to be able to perceive things accurately, at least with help.

Depressive illness responds much better to antidepressants plus therapy (particularly CBT) than to either alone. While the same can apply for very severe anxiety and panic states, this is only true to some extent. You need a degree of anxiety for the therapist to work on. If all your anxiety is covered over by the medication, there's nothing to work with. You can't experience, record and assimilate the experience of reducing anxiety through an effective relaxation technique, a systematic desensitization technique or a mindfulness procedure if you haven't got any. My view, therefore, is that while antidepressants can be used in anxiety states if absolutely necessary, it's worth trying to do without if possible. Not all my colleagues would agree with this; in fact I may be in the minority on this point. The SSRIs are used extensively to treat anxiety states.

Table 1 lists some of the antidepressants commonly used at the time of writing, with their characteristics. This list is not comprehensive, either in terms of the drugs cited, their effects or their side effects; it is a rough guide only. Please ask your doctor for more details.

Benzodiazepine Tranquillizers and Hypnotics

I am including here drugs that work on the same receptor systems in the brain, though they are of a different chemical structure from the original benzodiazepine drugs. The original benzodiazepines include diazepam (Valium), oxazepam and lorazepam, prescribed for anxiety, and nitrazepam and temazepam, prescribed for insomnia. The newer equivalent drugs include zopiclone (Zimovane), zolpidem

Table 1 Commonly Used Antidepressants

Drug Class	Drugs	Comments
Tricyclics	Amitriptyline, Dosulepin	Sedative. Side effects sometimes troublesome, e.g. dry mouth, blurred vision, dizziness, constipation, difficulty passing water, weight gain through increased appetite.
	Imipramine, Clomipramine	As above, but less sedative.
	Lofepramine	Side effects may be less than those above.
MAOIs	Phenelzine, Tranylcypromine	Food restrictions and drug interactions lead to these being infrequently used nowadays. Can be useful when other antidepressants don't work.
SSRIs (selective serotonin reuptake inhibitors – drugs acting on serotonin only)	Fluoxetine (Prozac)	All SSRIs can help with anxiety as well as depression. Side effects may include initial worsening of anxiety, headache, nausea (these three usually transient), vivid dreaming, sexual dysfunction. Prozac may be slightly appetite reducing. Sometimes slightly stimulant.
	Paroxetine (Paxil)	Slightly sedative, which can help with anxiety, but may be more difficult withdrawal (withdraw slowly, over several weeks).
	Citalopram (Celexa),	Usually quite easy to tolerate. Neither stimulant nor sedative.
	Escitalopram (Lexapro)	Lexapro may cause slightly less sexual dysfunction.
	Sertraline (Zoloft)	Slightly stimulant.
	Fluvoxamine (Luvox)	Less sexual dysfunction. More nausea and headache.

Drug Class	Drugs	Comments
Drugs acting on serotonin and noradrenaline (another transmitter chemical in the limbic system)	Venlafaxine (Effexor)	Sometimes works in depression when SSRIs haven't. Avoid in severe heart disease. Check blood pressure from time to time (can sometimes cause rise in BP).
	Duloxetine (Cymbalta)	May be safer in heart disease than Effexor. No significant effect on blood pressure.
	Mirtazapine (Zispin)	Sedative++, particularly at first. Weight gain through carbohydrate craving. No sexual dysfunction.

(Stilnoct) and zaleplon (Sonata). These drugs are highly effective in reducing anxiety and promoting sleep, but should only be used short term, because they are potentially addictive.

Benzodiazepines are also used as anaesthetics, detoxification agents, muscle relaxants and anti-epileptics; these uses are not discussed here. In terms of the applications I am dealing with, in my view these drugs should only be used in three situations. The first is when the degree of anxiety, panic or insomnia is so disabling that an urgent intervention is needed. They are a quickly effective remedy, giving those who are treating you a period of maybe up to two weeks to find a longer-term answer. Continuous usage of more than two weeks and you're looking at an ever-increasing risk of dependence. Second, they can be usefully employed on a basis of 'one in a crisis'. Nobody gets addicted if they are taking only one tablet every few weeks. Having a small supply in your handbag can give you sufficient reassurance that you feel calmer by their mere presence, meaning that you end up never taking them. Having said this, many cognitive therapists disapprove of such use, feeling that it detracts from your ability to manage your symptoms yourself. The third safe use is in specific occasional situations, such as allowing sleep on a transatlantic flight.

Don't rely on benzodiazepines to deal with your stress-related condition long term. They will only make it worse. I'll go further than that. If you see a new wonder drug advertised as the safe and non-addictive answer to anxiety and stress, don't believe it. I can trace back the history of 'non-addictive' anti-anxiety drugs which have subsequently been shown to be addictive at least 5,000 years. Any substance that holds out the promise of a stress-free existence is a fraud.

If you are already dependent on a benzodiazepine, though, don't panic. Most people are able to get off them without too much strife, with medical help, using a planned and supported slow withdrawal regime.

Buspirone

This drug, like the SSRIs, works on serotonin systems, but seems not to have a significant antidepressant effect. Whether it has significant advantages over the SSRIs in treatment of anxiety is a moot point, but at least it isn't significantly addictive in the way that benzodiazepines are.

Beta-Blockers

These drugs, particularly propranolol (Inderal), counteract some of the effects of adrenaline. While they don't get into the brain, they alleviate many of the unpleasant physical symptoms of anxiety. When you feel less anxious in your body, your mind tends to interpret your situation differently, reducing your fear, so unraveling the vicious cycle to some extent. These drugs can help some people and are non-addictive, but I wouldn't want to suggest that they are a solution to stress-related symptoms any more than any other drug.

Antipsychotics and Antihistamines

The older antipsychotic and antihistamine drugs are chemically related. As anyone who has taken Piriton for hayfever will know, some antihistamines are very sedative. This effect can be used to aid sleep without risking addiction. Nytol (diphenhydramine) and Phenergan (promethazine) are available over the counter without prescription. I wouldn't recommend the herbal form of Nytol, as I don't think it works. Antihistamines can be helpful for some, but they cause a bit of a hangover, so be careful if you have to drive the next day. In any case it's better not to rely on anything long term for sleep, as even non-addictive drugs will interfere with your natural sleep pattern if you rely on them every night.

Very small doses of antipsychotic drugs are sedative and slow your thinking down, so they can sometimes be useful in people tormented by anxious ruminations. While modern antipsychotic drugs don't have many of the side effects of the older compounds, they don't yet have a licence for use in treating anxiety or other stress-related conditions. This doesn't mean that they can't be used by experienced clinicians for such a purpose, but there isn't the body of experience in using them in these conditions that there is with other drugs on this list.

Pregabalin (Lyrica)

I include this drug here for completeness, but at the time of writing it has only just been promoted as a drug to treat anxiety, so I won't comment on it for or against. I may have more to say in a later edition of this book. It is primarily an anti-epileptic drug. I suspect that if it enjoys any success, a raft of other such drugs will hit the market shortly but I'm not waiting with bated breath. Drugs aren't a very big part of the solution to anxiety.

These are some of the treatments which should enable you to recover from this spell of illness, so long as you've rested enough. That's the first part done. The crucial part comes next: staying well. In order to achieve that, you are going to have to change the way you run your life. It isn't as complicated as you think, though, as I will now explain.

7

What You Can Do to Stay Well

Now here's the easy bit, at least in principle. We've done the hard work in going through the main causes of stress and its illnesses. Each of them have implications; ways in which they can be combated. Your task is to identify the causes that pertain to you. The remedial action then follows. Remember, *stress doesn't make you ill; you do.* While you may not be able to remove the stress which you are under completely, you have choices. Making the right ones will keep you well. If you've worked out what made you stressed, the steps you need to take are clear.

This chapter follows sections of earlier ones closely, as each cause of stress has its remedy. Just as the sections in the causes of stress chapters have links to the corresponding remedies in this chapter, each section here refers back to the corresponding cause(s).

Choosing Your Level of Arousal

(See page 4.)

Don't accept your life the way it is. You need to be able to own your life, to take responsibility for it. If you find yourself complaining a lot, feeling resentful, powerless, bored or overwhelmed, there are changes you need to make. These may cause some conflict, or require changes in your life, which will be stressful in themselves, but less so than letting a situation that is making you unhappy remain as it is. It's no good saying: 'I would love to have more time for myself but my husband won't have it', or: 'When I've done everything for the kids, there's nothing left for me.' By blaming them, you're avoiding taking responsibility for your own health and happiness. If everything that is required for you to satisfy the needs of your job, family, friends, house and the rest adds up to 100 percent of the time and energy available to you, it isn't an answer to say: 'Well, never mind about me, I don't matter, so long as everyone else is OK.' Everyone and everything will have to give a bit. You'll need to cut back on all these areas by 20 percent so that 20 percent of your life (minimum) is left for you. This is in everyone's interests, as you can stay well this way and be able to do more for them all in the long run than if you keep getting ill. It's no fun for them having you be ill, and it isn't necessary.

These changes will make you feel guilty. Don't worry about that. *Guilt is good.* It is a sign that you are making the changes you need to. Conversely, *resentment is bad.* It is an indication that you are sullenly, passively accepting the status quo. If nothing changes, everything remains the same. Is that your choice? If it isn't, change something. I can illustrate this another way, which may appeal to any mathematicians among you, with the following formula:

$$G - R > 0$$

G stands for guilt and R for resentment. In other words, your level of guilt needs to be greater than your level of resentment. If it is, you're making some of the changes you need to implement to stay well. If it isn't, you're not changing enough to give yourself a chance of achieving sustained health and happiness.

Your level of arousal needs to be sustainable. Life is a marathon, not a sprint. If you go at everything at 100 percent of your capacity, you'll be OK for a while, but when something comes up to put extra pressure and demands on you, you're in trouble. You need to have some reserve, to operate at just below the plateau of the Yerke-Dodson Curve (see p. 5). Fortunately the '98 for 60 principle' applies here. This rule has been pointed out to me by several of my patients in high-profile jobs or with demanding domestic situations who have got, and stayed, well. Give or take a few percentage points, they have all said the same thing: 'You know, I've realized that you can achieve 98 percent of the output with 60 percent of the effort. The disappointing part is that since my recovery, I've been coasting, and guess what – *nobody notices.* So what was it all for, all that busting my butt I used to do?' Good question.

Even in a very stressful environment, you achieve most by pacing yourself and prioritizing. Don't try to achieve everything all at once.

If you need to do more, to have more excitement in your life, do it. I know you have responsibilities and your spouse doesn't necessarily go along with your interests and preferred way of life. This is a time for compromise, to find a way in which your responsibilities and the needs of others can be balanced with your own needs. You don't have to keep everyone happy all the time. You matter too. If you need to take half a day a month to go parachute jumping, find a way to do so, by hook or by crook.

Managing Change

(See page 8.)

Change is stressful. First acknowledge that. If you try too hard to buy into the corporate or political enthusiasm for change, while also trying to do your real job and other roles to perfection, you'll get ill again. So a degree of cynicism is helpful here. Make the right noises, but pace yourself and recognize that if you have to change the way you do things, something has to give. Maybe the people or organization you serve isn't going to get all of you for a while, until it settles down and leaves you alone to do your job. Family and friends may have to accept a bit less of you for now too.

Maybe the changes will be for the best. Wait and see, but if they don't work out it isn't your fault. Don't try too hard to make the unworkable work.

If the changes are self-imposed, stick with them. Making choices involving change characterizes people who get happy and stay well, but only if they allow themselves to get it wrong sometimes. I'll expand on this a bit later. The key point here is the same for employers, politicians and individuals. Change, while sometimes necessary, causes temporary injury. The person undergoing major change needs to be treated like a patient recovering from major surgery: with care, gentleness, consideration and kindness, while he convalesces. And weigh up the risks and benefits before introducing further change in your organization. As it says in the Hippocratic oath: 'First, do no harm'.

Allowing Yourself to Fail

(See pages 10 and 19.)

Mistakes are great: they are the most potent agents for learning, if you use them correctly. It isn't easy to forgive mistakes if they have terrible consequences, as any loved one of a victim of a road accident or a serious medical error will tell you. But forgiving mistakes is crucial if real learning and improvement is to happen. This isn't to say that sloppiness and negligence should be condoned, only that even good, diligent people will get it wrong sometimes. The only way to avoid mistakes is never to try anything challenging or uncertain. That's a recipe for mediocrity and stagnation.

We are well aware nowadays that children should be allowed to experiment, make mistakes and be taught benignly through recognizing their errors and being kindly corrected. It's a shame that the trend for adults is in the opposite direction. For politicians 'accountability' means finding someone to punish, and I see too many good people making themselves ill through harsh self-criticism when things go wrong. Beware double standards. If you find yourself saying anything critical to yourself that you wouldn't say to another person in your situation, challenge the bully inside yourself: 'No, I'm not a stupid or pathetic person, I just made a mistake. It was understandable; I didn't know then what I know now. I made the best decision I could at the time, even if it's turned out wrong. So get off my back, bullying critic; you're wrong and I don't deserve it.'

And anyway, even if you have made a predictable mistake which could have been avoided, who hasn't? We should all be allowed to make errors sometimes. In my view it is the disappearance of this charitable response to personal failure that defines the present decline of our culture. Things get better (and people do too) if you let them sometimes get it wrong.

Try to get in the habit of challenging unfairly critical self-talk. If you couldn't persuade me of your guilt or worthlessness under vigorous challenge, then reject the thoughts. And look out for too many 'shoulds' and 'oughts'. If you find yourself thinking and saying these words a lot, you need to challenge your thinking (see later). These words, in excess, make you ill. Start thinking more about 'choose', 'want' and 'can'.

Everyone I've ever known who has been happy has been able to fail well. People who can try something, make a mess of it, learn and improve as a result, try again and carry on doing so until they get it right, become successful, multifaceted, interesting individuals. They are free to do whatever they want, unconstrained by the fear of failure. Think about it. Who do you know who is really happy? I'll bet he/she gets things wrong quite often and doesn't mind doing so. Failing well is arguably the most important skill a person can develop. It's a difficult one for the type of competitive, striving people who most often suffer from stress, but it's nonetheless crucial.

Coping with Excessive Demands

(See page 10.)

The keys here are realism and acceptance. It isn't fair that you are being asked to do twice as much with half the resources, but it's the way it is. So focus on the core tasks. Don't try to be everything to everyone. How will your performance be measured? Concentrate on those aspects of the job and let some other parts go a bit. Ensure that whatever you're doing is sustainable. It isn't an answer to work through the pain barrier for any but the shortest periods. Make sure you are delegating what you can, taking rest periods (even if that means you staying later), planning rather than just reacting, and keeping your main workplace as tidy as possible (my weak point). Always take lunch – you get more done if you do – but don't include alcohol in it.

Ensure, however busy you are, that you carve out time for leisure activities. Plan these and guard them with your life. Most of all, stop from time to time and be aware of your environment. Get outside and feel the breeze, smell the flowers (or the taxi fumes) and notice what is around you. Make a choice to include yourself in your life, right now, even when you've got a deadline to meet.

'But I haven't got any choice,' I hear you say. 'If I lose this job I won't be able to pay the mortgage and my wife will never forgive me', or: 'I'm a single mother with three kids under five, living in a two-bedroom apartment with no family or supports. I don't have any choices.' You do, but only if you accept your limitations. If you try to do the impossible, to be the best possible mother/employee/ whatever, in impossible circumstances, you'll get ill and that's in nobody's interests. Maybe the kids will have to spend a bit of time in front of the TV while you rest. Maybe you'll have to accept that you can't get the top appraisal this year. Or maybe you can't sort out your parents' housing right now, while the pressure is on at work. For once, you may need to let people be unhappy with you for not giving everything. That'll feel bad, but only for a bit, because you get used to anything, including accepting your limitations. If your self-esteem depends entirely on the approval of others, this will be hard, but not impossible. Talk to friends or others who are confident and good at setting limits. They'll give you good advice.

And then maybe you will lose your job or some other bad thing will happen. If you do, it isn't your fault. You can't avoid every misfortune in life. You took the choice that gave you the best chance of achieving sustainably the most you could. If that isn't enough, so be it. You can only do what you can do.

Here the serenity prayer, created by Alcoholics Anonymous (a wonderful group) comes in: '(God) Give me the serenity to accept what I can't change, the strength to change what I can change, and the wisdom to know the difference between the two.' Forgive me if I've changed any of the words, but that's the meaning and it works. Recognize where your sphere of influence ends. Practice the art of the possible. Stop banging your head against brick walls. There are things you *can* do; don't waste your time on what can't be done, once you've given it your best shot.

If you are a leader, beware asking too much of those you lead. You'll lose your best ones through stress-related illness and be left with the dross who have learned how to get around the system. Having said this, it's amazing how much people can achieve if they feel empowered. Talk to them, keep them informed and try to find a way of allowing them to take ownership of what they are doing. Of course, the buck stops with you and you can't consult everyone on every decision, but you can listen to their concerns and explain what is going on and why. That will increase their stress tolerance severalfold.

Staying in an Evolving Present

(See pages 12, 14 and 35.)

Suffering from the effects of stress requires two main errors: failing to live in the present and refusing to allow life to be. I explained this in the section 'Stress Is an Illusion' (p. 12). Learning how to experience what you are doing and witnessing now is in my view the most important skill a person can learn. It keeps you well and allows you sometimes to be happy. It is a central part of all philosophies relying on meditation, and of mindfulness, as I touched on in Chapter 6. It is also the message in the best-selling book *The Power of Now* by Eckhart Tolle.

Practice being vigilant for thoughts that center on the past or the future. While it's OK to plan, to reflect, to look forward or to acknowledge what has happened, this only works if it is a brief and occasional departure from experiencing what is happening now (except in grieving, which has to be allowed to happen for as long as it takes). If you are spending long periods ruminating about the past or the future, this is useless at best and harmful at worst. All that is real is going on now. Past misfortunes and mistakes are not under your control; try to consign them to your store of experience. The future will sort itself out if you deal with each present well; you can't do that if you aren't there because you are away in another time.

Check yourself on this every day and challenge yourself if you are falling away from the present. Whether you have a happy life doesn't depend on what you have got or will get right or wrong, but on how good you are at being kind to yourself when things go badly and how alive you become to each present experience.

This means letting life take whichever turn it chooses to, rather than pleading with it to do this or not to do that. Worrying about the future makes what you are worrying about no less likely to happen. If you are going to be blown up in a freak accident, you may as well get on and experience what you can before it happens (or doesn't happen). Life isn't a malicious trickster; it doesn't punish you for being happy or optimistic.

Try to observe your life rather than aiming to control it all the time. Let things change; look for the opportunities that changes bring, rather than dwell on the stresses you can't control. And let yourself change. There is no rule that you have to stay the same way, hold the same opinions, do the same things or seek the same goals forever. Are you really sure that you are doing what you want to do, what you choose? If not, change. If you are confused about what you want or who you are, talk about it as often and to as many people as you can. But then do what *you* want.

If you are someone who has undergone terrible trauma, particularly when you were very young, staying in the present will be very difficult. The mechanism you may have learned as a child, of imagining you are someone else/somewhere else/sometime else may have become very ingrained. When under stress, particularly of a type that reminds you of the past trauma, you may find yourself automatically switching off and your consciousness being removed from your present reality. You may even be aware of feeling and acting like a child frozen in your traumatized past, or as another person. But there is always a moment of choice, when you can choose to stay in the present. Try to identify these moments of choice and stay present. 'Dissociation', or the splitting off of your feelings from your present consciousness, doesn't do any good. Nothing changes and major problems tend to ensue. If you can't stay in the present, however hard you try, because of past trauma, you will need to seek some help. Go to your doctor first, who may refer you to a psychiatrist, psychologist or psychotherapist.

Dealing with Conflicting Needs

(See pages 15 and 16.)
Life seems very complicated at times. So often the demands on you are conflicting and you can't reconcile them. You are not able to keep everyone happy all the time, and however good you are somebody is going to criticize you for something sometime. But the longer I'm in this business, the more I come to believe that most things in life are simpler than they seem. We complicate issues by rationalizing our actions and mistakes, by trying to look good, to be perfect and by trying to make everything right.

It may be that there is no perfect solution to your problem. So find a course of action which does the least harm and/or the most good. If you can't decide what is best because there are too many uncertainties in your situation, make a decision anyway. Find a compromise if there is one. If there isn't, then decide and accept that you may be unfairly blamed; life and people are like that sometimes. But don't join in with the recriminations. You made the best decision you could at the time without the aid of retrospect.

I've become pretty good at finding this kind of balance. My publishers, lovely though they are, would have liked the manuscript for this book earlier. I know my limits and so chose to disappoint them rather than cause myself too much stress. I know my warning signs: palpitations and waking early in the morning. When these symptoms occur, publishers have to wait, my waiting list grows and some of my patients get a bit fed up. But that's the way it has to be. It's the best I can do, sustainably. Look out for your stress warning signs and then put your needs foremost. I can tell you, it's incredibly liberating when you stop trying to be everything for everybody and to sort everything out all the time.

Remember that you aren't responsible for the happiness of any other adult, not even your spouse. Of course you are responsible for being kind, considerate and (where appropriate) loving. Those are your actions; you can control them. But you aren't responsible for how they are received. If your attempt at kindness caused offense, it isn't your fault. Your benign action belongs to you, the offense belongs to the other person. People own their feelings; if you try too hard to take responsibility for them, their reactions and feelings, you are taking something that doesn't belong to you. Let people have their feelings, even if they are unhappy ones. Do good things for people, but not compulsively, to the exclusion of having a life.

Clear Communication

(See page 17.)

Say what you mean and what you need, at the time when you mean it and need it. Don't store things up. It is terrifically liberating to know that your loved ones are saying what they mean. If it hasn't been said, I don't have to worry about it. No hidden agendas, no hidden tripwires. I don't have to keep getting it wrong. Don't worry about being too demanding. Saying what you want gives the other person the opportunity to decline if they can't or don't want to do it. Try not to play games. Keep your communication clear, simple and honest. If your partner is playing games, bottling things up, or hiding her needs, call her on it.

Try to practice the art of negotiation. If you've never asked for things before, you won't do this very well at first. Don't worry, you'll get better at it over time. If you ask for something and your husband flatly refuses, don't leave it at that. Explore his reasons and make it clear that just brushing aside your wishes isn't in anybody's interests. 'Oh, you don't know my husband,' I hear you say. 'What he says goes; you can't argue with him.' But I'm not suggesting that you argue with him, just that you communicate your feelings and perceptions clearly:

'So you're just saying no, we can't go on vacation this year? Why not?'

'Because I'm too busy and we don't have the money.'

'Oh, OK, but then how come you're going on a 10-day golf holiday with your chums to Florida?'

'That was organized ages ago; I can't let them down.'

'I see. But I feel let down. I don't feel you're treating me as important as you and your friends.'

'Well, what do you expect me to do?'

'To give it some thought and do something to tell me I'm important. If it's only a long weekend in the mountains, maybe that'll have to do. But you come up with it. I need to know you can be bothered to think about me. It'll be in your interests to come up with something; I'll be much less grumpy.'

This type of exchange can lead to conflict, but not often, if you concentrate on talking about your feelings and needs, rather than making specific demands or attacking the whole person. It's OK to criticize a behavior and to ask for change, but attacking a person's character gets you nowhere. 'You're just a self-centered b****** and I hate you' tends to be counter-productive.

If your spouse/partner is just starting to assert her needs, do your best to listen and respond. Early attempts at asserting needs are a delicate flower, easily crushed. Soften your communication style as much as you can; life will be a lot happier for both of you if you do.

Watch couples who are good at negotiating and learn from them. Don't blame your partner if it isn't working; it's up to you to keep pushing for what you need.

Allow your partner to be the sex he/she is. Recognize his/her strengths and tendencies and work with them. Don't expect your husband to be an honorary woman, sensitive to feelings and needs, like your girlfriends are (unless he is). Tell him what you need, several times over if necessary. Don't expect your wife to focus dispassionately on the practical solutions to the situation without grappling with the emotional aspects for a while (unless she does). Spend some time letting her tell you about how she feels.

And most of all, don't 'right fight'. There is no right and or wrong in feelings; they're just feelings. Allow each other to have different views, needs and feelings. Don't demand that your partner see things the way you do. Focus more on understanding what he/she thinks and feels than on stating and restating your position. You don't have to accept that you're wrong, just acknowledge the other view.

But however many mistakes you make in your communication, any talking is better than none, at least to most people. I once had a patient who I had treated for stress, caused in part by marital problems. I lost touch with him when I moved jobs, but met him again when I returned a few years later. 'How's your marriage?' I asked. 'Great,' he replied. 'Does your wife agree?' I inquired. 'I've no idea, I haven't spoken to her for a year.' He was quite happy, as his wife was quietly doing things for him; but she was by that time being treated herself for a severe depressive illness.

It's good to talk; make sure you do it often and try to focus on the positives. When was the last time you praised and expressed your appreciation of your partner, your friend, your employee or the lady who gives you coffee at the station with such a nice smile? Positive feedback is one of the greatest gifts you can give, and as a rule the more you give the more you receive.

And make sure to seek out the humor in your life. Laughter is a potent stress-reliever. There's plenty to laugh about. Just look at the government—what a scream!

Minimizing Value Judgements

(See page 21.)

Having some values is, of course, part of being a civilized person. But make sure that you only impose these judgements when you need to and that you don't employ double standards.

I've already advised that you monitor your own thinking. Look out for the sort of self-deprecation that is just plain unkind. If you wouldn't say it about someone else, don't say it to or about yourself. You really need a friend right now. Be one to yourself. You don't need abuse, so don't allow yourself to heap opprobrium on your head. It isn't kind or fair. If you're the sort of person who enjoys going around criticizing other people and humiliating them, then, be my guest, give yourself the hardest time you can. I have no time for you the way you are and I wouldn't want to know you. But I don't think so; if you were like that, you wouldn't have been affected by stress. Lots of people around you would have been, but not you.

No, you're someone who tries hard and wants to do the right thing. So stop using words like 'weak', 'pathetic', 'ought' and 'should' about yourself. Let yourself learn from experience without fear of criticism.

Alcohol and Drugs

(See page 22.)

Sorry, but you're not going to get better if you take illicit drugs, and that's the final word. That includes cannabis. If you are determined to continue using, this book is wasting your time. Tear out the pages and use them to wrap your joints in.

If you're using tranquillizers, you do need to get off them, but not all of a sudden. Go and see your doctor. Don't just stop taking them, as that will only make things worse. If the withdrawal process is done slowly and methodically, it doesn't have to be hard. If you're on antidepressants, stay on them until your doctor tells you to phase them out. Coming off too soon can cause an unnecessary problem.

Most likely, your drug of choice is alcohol. It worked so well at first. But you won't get and stay well unless you can get down to normal limits. Use the units system for this. One unit is equal to:

- 1 small glass of wine (8 units in a bottle)
- 1 pub measure of spirits (30 units in a .7 L bottle)
- Half a pint weaker beer (3–4%)
- Third of a pint stronger beer (5% or more)
- 1 small glass of sherry/port

	Monday	Tuesday	Wednesday	Thursday	Friday	Saturday	Sunday
Lunchtime		2		2		4	4
Evening	3	4	3 before dinner				
			4 at dinner		6	6	
			3 after dinner				
Total units	3	6	10	2	6	10	4

Weekly total units = 41

Figure 3 A drink diary from *Dying for a Drink* by Dr. Tim Cantopher, The Book Guild, 1996

Keep a drink diary. Figure 3 is an example of one. You record your units as you consume them. Keep your notepad in your pocket/ handbag at all times. At the end of the day total up your day's consumption. On Sunday evenings you have the joyous task of working out your weekly total.

If this is below 28 units a week for a man, or 21 units a week for a woman, you're OK and within safe limits. (This is sometimes disputed; recent guidance is to keep within daily limits, because of the trend to binge-drink, and some authorities recommend weekly totals of 21 and 14 units for men and women respectively.) There are exceptions, such as pregnancy, when levels of drinking should be much lower. If you drink over 50 units a week as a man, or 35 units a week as a woman, your drinking is a major part of your problem. To get better you'll have to bring your drinking down to safe levels first. If you are physically dependent (daily heavy drinking, with morning shakes, getting worse if you don't drink through the day), you need urgent medical attention. Don't just stop, as that could be dangerous. In any case, if you are struggling to control your drinking, go and see your doctor.

Controlling your drinking won't help immediately. In fact, you may feel worse for a little while. But if you persevere, you'll start to feel better within a few days to a few weeks.

Balance and Exercise

(See page 24.)
Three questions separate those of my patients who stay well once they have recovered, from those who keep getting ill. They are:

- What do *I* want (not, what does everyone else think I should want)?
- What's it all for anyway (all this stuff that I do)?
- Where is the balance in my life?

This balance covers all sorts of areas, for example the work–life balance, the balance between your needs and the needs of others, between time spent on tasks and recreation and between the two needs for exercise and rest. Exercise is a powerful stress reliever. Use it regularly, but not to the exclusion of time spent just relaxing – sitting around doing nothing much. If you can't just sit around, you're over-aroused. You need to spend more time on learning a relaxation exercise.

A balanced diet may also be a factor. It certainly reduces the health risks of stress, though I must say I think the potential for dietary changes to treat stress-related psychological conditions is a bit over-hyped nowadays.

Changing Your Personality

(See page 27.)
Right now, when you are trying to get better or are in the process of recovery, *your actions are more important than your feelings*. That doesn't mean that you should just soldier on, denying your feelings and putting on a brave face. It does mean that *you become the way that you act*, so to change the way you are – your personality – make the right moves. As they say in AA, 'fake it to make it'.

As personality is a product of your behaviors, to change it you need to change the way you behave. This may need to be done slowly. If you find that there is something you need to do, but you are avoiding doing it, it's no good just beating yourself up for being lazy. You aren't lazy; there's a good reason you aren't doing it. It may be fear, because during the time that you've been ill and withdrawn you've become phobic of the task. It may be that you are expecting too much of yourself, planning to sort out a major issue at too early a stage of your recovery. Your body is telling you: 'Don't do this thing, it will hurt you.' That's because the way you've planned it, as one big task, it will. You need to pace yourself. Either way, the answer is to start slowly: do what you have been avoiding a bit at a time, being kind to yourself and avoiding beating yourself up for not doing more. Your inactivity is a result of expecting too much of yourself, not too little. So don't stay as you are, but don't do too much either.

Let me give an example. Say you are avoiding social situations because they scare you. While the only way you are going to get more confident socially, or to regain the confidence you've lost, is to have more contact with people, you shouldn't try to do this all of a sudden. Don't go to a lot of parties, or volunteer to be parent–teacher rep. Start with having a friend over for coffee, or go with a friend or your partner for lunch, so that you get used to the hustle and bustle of public places. Once you've achieved this, try a bit more, such as going to a parents' meeting at your child's school, but not contributing yet; that comes later. And so on. The same principle holds whatever your circumstances are. Take it slowly and steadily.

Do a bit more than what comes easily, but not enormously so. Then don't expect yourself to do it well. You won't be the world's greatest conversationalist for a while yet. Treat yourself kindly along the way. If you keep the process of doing a bit more each time going, you'll eventually feel at ease in social situations. You'll become a social person. Your personality will have changed. This process works, if you do it slowly, and avoid judgement and criticism of yourself. And remember, you're only responsible for what you do, not for the reaction of others. So if you try to come out of yourself by saying hello to one of your child's friend's mothers at the school gate, only to have her ignore you, that isn't a failure, but a triumph. You did what you needed to do. Her reaction was irrelevant, because if you keep coming out of yourself this way, you'll develop friendships before you know it. (Incidentally, she probably had a fight with her husband the night before – the chances are her apparent rudeness had nothing to do with you.)

Gaining an Accurate View of Yourself, the World and the Future by Challenging Negative Thinking

(See pages 19, 29, 34 and 37.)

This is the basis of cognitive therapy (CBT), which I touched on in the last chapter. Stress only hurts you if you try to overcome the unovercome-able or if you perceive it as threatening. So if you aren't going to do a course of CBT, you need to do less and challenge your perceptions and way of thinking more. Let me return to the example I gave in Chapter 2 about the people facing layoffs. John wasn't being unrealistic in thinking that he would escape unaffected, or if not that something else would come along. Why shouldn't it? Life isn't conspiring to bring you down. Paul, expecting to meet a catastrophe, is being fanciful in the extreme. If, rather than focusing on his fear, he concentrated on doing his job, he would probably escape the axe. If he does lose his job, he is very unlikely not to find another job and even less likely to face starvation. Paul needs to challenge his thinking, or talk to others who can challenge it for him.

You are the way you are for good reasons. *It isn't your fault.* The way you act, think and feel is a result of your childhood (and to a lesser extent later) experiences. Maybe your parents forgot to approve of you as a child, didn't give you the love and warmth you so needed, used you instead of nurturing you. Maybe other people or losses early in life taught you that the world isn't a safe place where things turn out all right in the end. Maybe bullies, be they peers or teachers, taught you to fear. Maybe there was no consistency in your childhood experiences and perhaps your life has been a succession of disappointments, rejections and losses ever since. Maybe you never learned that you are OK, just because you are you. As a result, you run your life as a series of tasks to achieve, people to please, obligations to fulfill and disasters to avoid.

That's fine when everything's going well, but when life throws you insoluble problems or someone turns nasty, you try to fix the unfixable. Your stress level rises. You get ill.

As likely as not, you are ashamed for being the way you are. You feel that other people cope with more than you do and manage better. You realize that you don't feel for others as you should, because you're so preoccupied with how they see you and with getting approval. You feel that you are self-obsessed, caught up with your own insecurity, and you wish you were like those people who seem to find it so easy to be interested in others. But I mean it: *it isn't your fault*. The first step to changing is becoming a benign and loving parent or teacher to yourself. Allow yourself to be, then try changing the way you act, as I've already explained. Don't do, or expect of yourself, what you wouldn't expect of others.

I told you earlier in this book of the horrible teacher who made learning so frightening and difficult for me and my peers in primary school. But there were others whose wonderful kindness energized and encouraged us. Taught by the likes of Father Bruno, Father Bernard (it was a Catholic school), Mr. Freeland and Mr. Garry, we were encouraged to explore our capabilities, to have fun, to make mistakes, to learn. We felt we could fly. To them and to my wonderful parents go the credit for any creativity I have and any help I am able to give others. My parents taught me that I was the most important person alive. I think that led to me becoming a fairly bumptious and unpleasant adolescent, but through my teens my friends and others knocked the spots off me and I learned to be a bit less pompous. But the inner certainty remains: 'I'm OK.' This helps a lot when life turns hostile. If a patient praises me (which is very welcome) it doesn't change the way I view myself much; I know my strengths and weaknesses and have accepted them, though I do try to improve and keep learning. If a patient criticizes me, I try to learn from what they say, but it also doesn't affect my view of myself. This allows me to do my job focusing on the needs of my patients, not on a need for short-term approval or success.

So if you haven't been taught early on that you're OK, the world is OK, the future is OK, to accept yourself the way you are, what are you to do? First, recognize that what applies to a child also applies to you. If a child doesn't achieve anything when bullied, but learns and grows when taught kindly, with encouragement and patience, the same is true for you. Be kind in your talk to yourself. Try to be aware of what you are saying to yourself, assess whether it is fair (would you say it to another person in your situation?) and kind, and challenge it vigorously if it isn't. Bullies have to be stood up to, or they will demolish you. Stand up to the bully (only of yourself) inside you.

Challenging ingrained negative thinking patterns isn't easy. It takes a lot of practice. Even becoming aware of your negative thoughts is quite hard, as they become so ingrained over time. So to start with, your task is to become more aware. Put a lot of effort into identifying the negative thoughts that charac-terize your thinking. Write them down in a notebook on the spot, linking them to the events that triggered them. Carry the notebook with you. Note how these thoughts make you feel and any symptoms that result. Write those feelings and symptoms down too. How does that affect your mood? Rate your mood out of 10 before and following the thought, with 0 being the worst you've ever felt and 10 the best. You'll quickly come to see how events trigger negative thoughts and how these lead to lowered mood and other symptoms.

I think that recognizing these thought processes is the trickiest part. Once you see the patterns, the thought processes become open to challenge; they stop being automatic. If they are just mean, you can throw them out. In any case, they can be studied.

For any such negative thoughts, see if you can identify a pattern to them. Is there an underlying assumption? Examples of common assumptions are: I'm no good, I'll be found wanting, things will always go wrong in the end, there's a disaster around the corner (particularly if I ever allow myself to be happy or optimistic), life will play a trick on me unless I'm in control all the time, nobody will like me and I'm only as good as what others say about me/what I can do for others.

When you've gotten used to this process, start challenging the thoughts and assumptions. For each thought, generate some alternative thoughts and assumptions, with the evidence for them. Try rating their relative probabilities, in percentage terms. Then test out the hypotheses in practice. Once you've done this, redo your rating of probability and consciously accept the most probable interpretation. Finally, rate your mood again and note the difference in how this process has made you feel. Do this process over and over again, whenever you notice yourself feeling bad and thinking negatively. Get someone close to you to help with the process by giving another view, if possible.

You are now your own cognitive therapist. Eventually you'll get so good at challenging your thoughts on the spot that you won't need the notebook any more, and your underlying assumptions will change. This can change your life. It's worth the effort. Let me give a simple example: Your boss ignores you when you are passing him in the corridor at work. Your notebook may look like Table 2a.

Table 2a A Sample Thought Record

Event	Thoughts	Feelings/symptoms	Mood before and after	Assumptions
Boss ignored me.	He's angry with me, he thinks I'm no good, I'll lose my job, my family will starve.	Anxious, sad, sinking feeling in stomach, feel sick.	6/10 before 1/10 after	

To begin with, the assumptions column will be empty. After going through this process a number of times, you'll recognize a pattern emerging and will be able to recognize the assumptions (see Table 2b).

Table 2b A Sample Thought Record with Assumptions

Event	Thoughts	Feelings/ symptoms	Mood before/after	Assumptions
Boss ignored me.	He's angry with me, he thinks I'm no good, I'll lose my job, my family will starve.	Anxious, sad, sinking feeling in stomach, feel sick.	6/10 before 1/10 after	I'm no good. I'll always be found wanting. There's a disaster around the corner.

Table 3   A Sample Thought Challenge Record

Thought and alternatives	Evidence	Probability	Test and result	New probability	Mood now
Boss is cross with me.	He ignored me.	80%	Emailed to ask him if my last project was OK. He emailed back that it was fine.	5%	
He noticed something/ someone else and didn't see me.	He was looking through the window at something outside.	10%		5%	7/10
He was distracted by some-thing that happened recently.	He looked distracted.	10%	Spoke to colleague in office next to him who heard him arguing with his wife half an hour before.	90%	

After you've got used to this process, you add in a second set of headings on the facing page in your notebook, for each such event (see Table 3). Of course, sometimes it isn't possible to test your alternative hypotheses out. Instead, talk to someone about them, or imagine that you're discussing them with me. Try to cross-examine yourself to make sure your logic stands up. If not, alter the probabilities as I've demonstrated.

You'll soon get used to this process and be able to do it really quickly. It works. But to do so, your changing way of thinking needs to lead to a different way of operating.

If you spend most of your time rushing around after others because you crave their approval, assuming that you have no worth, this thought and assumption needs to be challenged. Doing so will only help you, though, if it leads to you no longer putting the need to please others above all else. Changed thinking has to be combined with changed actions. This applies most of all with parents. You are responsible for yourself first and them only second. You need to put down some boundaries, particularly if they demand a lot of you. More of that shortly.

You may need some help with this. If you can't get or haven't the time for a course of CBT, try reading *The Feeling Good Handbook* (David D. Burns), or the shorter *How to Make Yourself Miserable* (Windy Dryden). Or ask your doctor to recommend self-help literature or websites (these are changing all the time).

Taking Emotional Risks

(See pages 29, 32 and 37.)

If you have learned to be helpless, if life has habitually kicked you when you are down, there won't seem much point in reaching out for happiness. Your tendency will be to be satisfied with avoiding disasters. But where does that lead? If you're lucky you'll look back in your old age and be able to say: 'I didn't have many disasters.' So what? That's not a life. Most of the happiest people I have met have had plenty of disasters in their lives, but they have accepted them and not let misfortune deflect them from seeking what they want in life.

It isn't whether your first love returns your devotion that determines whether you have a happy life or not (though it seems so at the time), but whether you are able to give it a go, to make yourself vulnerable by declaring your affection for her. If she rejects you, it hurts like blazes, but if you do exactly the same thing the next time you fall in love, and the next, in the face of the risk of rejection, I guarantee, you'll find happiness in the end. This is true because positive relationships are the way most people find happiness and they reduce the harmful effects of stress. It's also true of other emotional risks, for example in making changes to the way you lead your life. Making active decisions, regardless of whether they turn out well, leads to you feeling more effective and in control of your environment. This in turn leads to you experiencing less stress. This is a point for employers to remember too: more empowerment leads to less stress and greater productivity.

So take emotional risks. Allowing yourself to be hurt leads to happiness. But don't keep going for the benefit of people who hurt you (see later).

Dealing with Trauma and Loss

(See pages 35 and 37.)

There's no way around bereavement, other losses and traumas; they're horrid. They hurt, and the feelings go on for so long. But there is an end to them, so long as you *let yourself feel*. That isn't to say that it's ever OK that you've lost your loved one, or that you're suffering so terribly; it isn't, and never will be. It's just that if you let yourself feel, to acknowledge and experience your grief or hurt, you will, in time, become free – free to feel your sadness or pain when you choose to feel it, instead of it punching you in the gut at every turn, or at the most inopportune times. I remember, when my brother died (I was 24), I felt nothing much at first and several people remarked how jolly I was at the wake. Then six months later it pole-axed me. My housemates got very fed up with my moping, feeling that I should have gotten over it by then. That isn't the way grief works; it takes as long as it takes. But if you feel it, you get to the point at which you feel other emotions too. You become free to feel happiness, excitement, love, anger, boredom, interest and any other emotion depending on circumstances, as well as feeling sad when you choose to do so.

If you don't let yourself feel, you get trapped and frozen, with the grief or trauma lurking, waiting to be awakened by events or circumstances which resonate with it (which remind you of it), leading to a double dose of feelings which can be even harder to tolerate.

The only thing to do with feelings, however difficult, is to feel them. They won't hurt like this for ever.

Dealing with Toxic People and Places

(See page 29 and Chapter 4.)

I've left the most important section until last. But complicated though these people make your life, this section isn't very long, because there isn't much to say, other than this: set boundaries, be clear on your limits, and if they continue to hurt you, consider whether they should be part of your life.

You can't beat some toxic people, because they're better at hurting people than you are at fighting them; they've been doing it all their lives. You can't change them if they don't want to change because they don't believe they have a problem. It's no use appealing to their better nature, because they haven't got one. If you try to put on limits, to have boundaries in your dealings with them, they will ignore and invade them.

So, first identify these takers, tell them what needs to change, and if they don't, get away from them. When you do so, though, mark my words, they will try to reel you back in. All of a sudden, the person who has been so mean and had no time for you will be all over you like a rash and full of enticing promises. Don't be fooled: if you let them back into your life, they will use you and hurt you just like before. They're only being nice to get you back because they need you. If you still resist, next they'll try to persuade you that it's your fault, that you need them, and without them nobody else will want to know you. But they're lying. There are lots of good people out there who are generous of spirit and will give as well as take. Once you weed out the toxic people, you'll find that these givers start appearing in increasing numbers and you'll begin to get more out of life. So, scary though it is, take a deep breath and do it. Give your address book a cleanout.

With family, of course, it's a lot more difficult. I won't suggest that you cut yourself off completely from your parents, siblings or children unless there is no other choice. And I'm not advocating separation or divorce unless everything else has been tried. A start here is to recognize that it isn't you who has been the problem. While your father may be telling you that you are selfish and uncaring because you won't go around every day to help him, the truth is that selfish and uncaring people don't get stress-related illness, so he's wrong. Indeed, the fact that you are feeling so guilty suggests that he failed to teach you in your formative years that your needs and welfare are paramount. He should have done that, it's what parents are for; the demanding behavior he's exhibiting now is just another manifestation of the self-centeredness that led to him ignoring your needs earlier in your life. But if you choose to keep dancing to his tune, it's not his fault, it's yours; you're choosing to be a victim. Make another choice – decide for yourself how much you choose to give him and then stick to it. He'll make you feel guilty, but that's a good sign. Guilt is good. It means that you're changing the habits of a lifetime and standing up for yourself. If you don't know how much to do for him, ask someone who knows you both. Don't ask someone who is only friendly with you or him, because they will give you polarized and partisan advice. It's too easy to dismiss the needs and motives of someone you don't know.

Once you've decided on your boundaries, stick to them, through thick and thin. And hold onto your hat, it'll be a bumpy ride. Your limits will be tested to the limit.

This is sometimes very difficult. Don't be hard on yourself if you let your boundaries slip, or get drawn back in. It happens. These people are awfully good at manipulation, so the wisest and strongest of us often need a few stabs at getting it right. Keep trying.

And beware of mistaking illness for bad behavior. If your friend, partner, spouse or other family member has inexplicably changed for the worse, don't abandon them, but get medical help.

Organizations are even harder to change than individuals. That doesn't mean that it's not worth trying. My own view is that our whole country has been made toxic by our politicians and elements of the press. I take every chance I am given to resist them, but at the same time I'm a realist. I don't suppose that our leaders are quaking in their boots in the knowledge that I despise them. I do what I can, but then I accept my powerlessness and look for what I can achieve and the joy that is within my grasp.

Accepting the limits to what you can change may allow you to stay in your present company, organization or group. If you can learn to just shrug and just get on with what you want to do, accepting the inadequacies of the organization while insulating yourself from them as far as you can, you may find that you can exist within it quite happily. But don't wait for it to change, because it is very unlikely to do so. If you can't change it, but you can't accept it, you should leave. This may be a risk, but the vast majority of people who get out of toxic organizations are happier and healthier as a result, however poor they may be in the short term. If you really can't leave because of being financially trapped, then find a way to give less, so that you can expand other more rewarding areas of your life.

The prizes for ejecting the toxic people and places from your life, once the short-term guilt and anxiety has passed, are health and happiness. I can tell you from personal experience, it is so liberating when you start being able to say no to people, and stop trying to make everyone like and approve of you. It's freedom.

8

Kill Your Stress with Kindness

This book has been a bit of a race, hasn't it? How to deal with the problems of human existence in a hundred pages. Not possible, but I've done my best to pass on what my patients have taught me about what has made them ill and what to do about it. Most of them come to me feeling that they are trapped, with no choices, stuck in a life of torment with no way out. But that's because they assume that they are responsible for everything and everyone and are uniquely to blame for everything that goes wrong around them. They've built their own prison through their givens: 'It's a given that we have to stay in this house, that the kids have to go to private school and that I have to take Mom to the shops three times a week.'

No, it isn't. Are you going to die of exposure if you move to a smaller house? Are the kids going to perish if they move back to public schools? Does Mom have no friends or access to services who can help out with her shopping? Give me a break. You've got choices, you just haven't been prepared to take them because you are determined that you've got to do it all. Perfectly and beyond reproach. If that means driving yourself to an early grave following a life devoid of joy, that's a price you've been prepared to pay. But is it really, or have you just been careering through life at a million miles an hour without really thinking about it?

So stop and think. Is that really what you want? If not, make some changes, maybe along the lines I have suggested in the previous chapter.

Sometimes through therapy, sometimes just through thought and talking with me and others who care about them, many of my patients come to realize that they do have choices, and they choose to stop being so mean to themselves. They start looking for balance and take a bit more for themselves. For a while, some friends and family moan a bit, because they have lost the unpaid servant they had gotten used to. But in the long run, if they care about you, they come to appreciate the joy, the humor, the expanding love, that results from a person less weighed down by tasks and other stress. As often as not, while they see you doing a bit less for them, they notice that you've become *kinder* – less irritable, less judgemental, more able to notice and appreciate them.

You will have noticed the theme of kindness being repeated many times throughout this book. That's because, in my view, it's the number one key to health and happiness. It won't be lost on you that it is the central message in the Christian tradition, but that is true in many other religions and philosophies as well. Kindness works. Most of my patients don't need to be told this; they are the best and kindest people around. Except to themselves. A few are unkind to everyone. In any case, it doesn't work. If you are cruel or harsh to your employees, they will perform poorly and your business will fail. If you are habitually horrible in shops, you will get poor service. If you pick fights with your neighbors, you'll get nothing but coldness and obstructiveness in return. I could go on, but there's no point. You know that it's more efficient to be kind to others. But to yourself? I don't think so.

So am I wrong? Maybe you should continue to have double standards, to berate, push and deny yourself in a way in which you would never consider treating anyone else. I can't see it, though. I don't understand who gains from it, in the long run. Your family and friends get someone who is miserable, exhausted and irritable for now, then ill and unable to function at all. If it goes on they will lose you before your time. Meanwhile, their opportunity to learn from their own experience and assumption of responsibility is taken away, because you do everything including all the worrying. I don't think it makes sense or does anyone any good to carry on this way.

Kindness to yourself works. It's difficult to do, but becomes easier with practice. When you get the hang of it, as a result you are more productive, more fun, more help, more healthy and more happy. If this makes sense to you, ask yourself every day, just before bed: 'Have I been as kind to myself today (in what I've said to myself and the way I've treated myself) as I try to be to others?' If not, what can you do differently tomorrow?

Do you remember Steve, from the beginning of this book? It's ironic that he should have been the one to storm off to lynch the station manager, because he's actually one of the kindest people I know. At least he is to others – although not on the golf course, where he's as mean as a Scottish miser. Anyway, one day, by chance, I met the station manager in question at Wentworth golf course. He and a friend had been paired with Steve and me to play in a foursome. As he approached, Steve told me who he was. I was appalled, foreseeing a tense round at best, and physical violence at worst. Not so Steve – at the tee the two greeted each other as long-lost friends.

It transpired that when Steve arrived at the manager's office on the day of the big delay, he was just clocking off after a very stressful week, when almost everything had gone wrong. He hadn't made any passenger announcements on that day because there had been an incident the details of which he had been forbidden to communicate to the public. He was stressed and powerless, and Steve was stressed and powerless. So what did they do? They went and had a beer, listened to each other's frustrations, had a meal, then shared a taxi back to the town where they discovered they both lived. From what they told me on the golf course, they had had a lovely evening. Each was at pains to tell me how kind the other had been in the difficult circumstances that had prevailed that afternoon in London. Funny thing, life – once you stop fighting it, it seems to get better.

Index

CPSIA information can be obtained at www.ICGtesting.com
Printed in the USA
LVOW10s2347300915

456416LV00014B/102/P